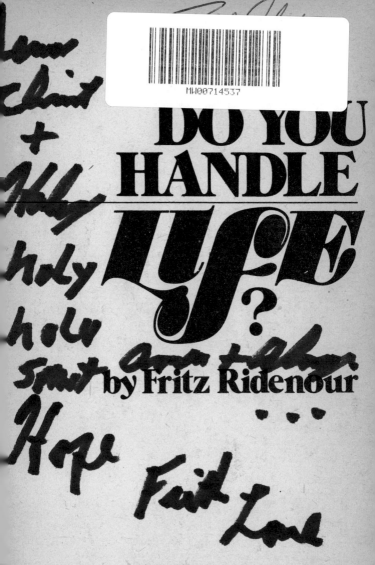

DO YOU HANDLE LIFE?

by Fritz Ridenour

A Division of G/L Publications
Glendale, California, U.S.A.

[Handwritten annotations:] love christ + Holy, holy, holy Spirit, Hope, Faith Love

Over 130,000 in print

Second Printing, 1971
Third Printing, 1972
Fourth Printing, 1973
Fifth Printing, 1975
Sixth Printing, 1976
Seventh Printing, 1977
Eighth Printing, 1977

Published by
Regal Books Division, G/L Publications
Glendale, California 91209

Printed in U.S.A.

Originally published under the title *Take Your Choice.*

Library of Congress Catalog No. 77-140941
ISBN 0-8307-0430-2

CONTENTS

A teaching and discussion guide for use with this book is available from your church supplier.

The Choices Are Always A Few Minutes Ahead

Decisions . . . decisions . . . how do you make them in a world that is changing so fast? What you decide this morning can be obsolete, overruled or completely "out of it" by nightfall.

We're all gasping for breath. We're not necessarily asking them to stop the world so we can get off. We'd be happy if they would just slow the thing down so we could catch up.

But we can't catch up. Incredible revolutions in science, government, education—social developments of all kinds—are set in motion and nothing (on this planet at least) can stop them.

There's a revolution in religion too. People—young and old—are on the march. The church is being criticized as part of an oppressive establishment that cares only about perpetuating itself, not meeting the needs of human beings.

Inside the church, and out, the clamoring critics are candid and—in many cases—correct.

So what's to be done? Should believers in Christ—His church—admit God is dead and commit suicide on His grave?

Not on your protest sign . . .

There's still that little item called faith.

Christians are people who have faith in Christ. It was faith that caused Peter to tell Jesus that He was "The Messiah, the Son of the living God." To which Christ replied, "Upon this rock (your faith) I will build My church; and all the powers of hell shall not prevail against it" (see Matt. 16:15-18).

Keeping the faith isn't going to take away the mind-boggling problems of the late twentieth century. (Sometimes having faith increases them.) But Jesus

Christ is our *problem solver*—if we have faith enough to let Him.

When it comes to "living the Christian life" in this anything-but-Christian world, we constantly face choices and so did those who walked and talked with Jesus Christ. This book lets you see some basic choices in life through the eyes of New Testament people like John the Baptist, Lazarus, Mary and Martha, Peter, Stephen, Paul, Barnabas, Thomas and Timothy. Life may have been simpler then, but the choices were the same as they are now:

. . . Doubt Christ or keep coming to Him—even when you're not sure He is who He said He was.

. . . Fear death (always on the horizon in the shape of that mushroom cloud), or face it with the hope that you can never die.

. . . Keep ducking the prejudice issue with sour grapes ("They're happier with their own kind"), or realize that God settled the race question quite awhile ago and it's time you caught up.

. . . Remain one of the vast Christian silent majority, or start sharing your beliefs in what you say and what you do.

. . . Write off the losers in life (there are so many of them), or start reaching out to some of them at least to give them another chance.

. . . Self-righteously protect the subculture on your side of the generation gap, or let the Holy Spirit close that gap with a little good old-fashioned Christian discipline.

It's a world of change and a world of choices. The change is upon us. The choices are always just a few minutes ahead, and we have to make many every day. God's prophet Elijah put it this way: "How long will you sit on the fence?"

So, read on—and decide how you will handle life.

FRITZ RIDENOUR
G/L Publications

CHAPTER 1

DON'T KNOCK *IT* BeFoRe YOU ReaLLY TRY *HIM*

Beatle Ringo Starr arrived in Los Angeles to plug his new movie, *The Magic Christian*, a tongue-in-cheek critique of the establishment and Christian values. While being interviewed for a local radio newscast, Ringo had a few comments on Christianity, which centered around the idea that the Christian church has "blown it" because it hasn't shared its great wealth with all of the poor people of the world.

With assurance and conviction, Ringo pinpointed the hypocrisy of the church with what he thought was devastating accuracy. (He did not pinpoint just how much of *their* great wealth the Beatles were sharing with the poor.)

Unfortunately, there are people who agree with Ringo's limited logic. They somehow equate Christianity with a cure-all for all the evils of the world. And because all the evils of the world aren't solved, they blame Christians for fouling up the detail.

"We're more popular than Jesus now"—J. Lennon

Some people claim that Christianity is one of the chief causes of the many ills we have today. Others nodded in agreement when Ringo's partner, John Lennon, uttered his legendary put-down: "Christianity will go. It will vanish and shrink. I needn't argue about that; I'm right, and I will be proved right. We're more popular than Jesus now; I don't know which will go first—rock 'n' roll or Christianity."[1]

These acid (no pun intended) remarks out of the mouths of Beatles are representative of a widespread discontent with the brand of Christianity practiced by many Christians today. There is a general feeling that if God did manifest Himself to the world in Jesus Christ, then why hasn't the church gotten just a little better grip on things after 2,000 years of being in business?

But are the Beatles and other critics of Christianity correct? Do they have the real picture? Are they "right on"? A little bit off? Or out to lunch? After all, 2,000 years is a long time to be in business. Has Christianity merely dispensed a product called the Gospel without being in touch with people and their needs?

First, it might help to ask if Christianity "started

as a business." Did an itinerant rabbi from Nazareth appear one day in Jerusalem and nail up his shingle and set up his shop? Whenever you talk about any person or group or organization it's always a good idea to "consider the source." From where did Christianity spring? Under what circumstances? Into what kind of world did Christianity come and *why?*

For one thing, Christianity came into a world that was fed up with "religious business as usual." It was a world that worshiped gods of all assorted kinds. The great empires that had ruled most of the known population of the earth in the centuries before Christ all had their gods. And most of the people of the world were still held in the grip of pagan polytheism—especially the brand that had come out of Greek mythology and Roman worship of the state.

Oh yes, there was that small segment of humanity called the Jews who claimed they believed in Yahweh—the one true God—or so they said. But the history of the Jews was so checkered with apostasy and periods of slipping into pagan idolatry that it was hard to believe they had the real answer. Furthermore, in the centuries just prior to the coming of Christ, the Jews more than anyone else seemed hung up on making their religion into a system of rules, laws and traditions.

There had to be a better way than "religion"

There was . . . and still is.

". . . When the right time finally came, God sent

His own Son. He came as the son of a human mother, and lived under the Jewish Law, to set free those who were under the Law, so that we might become God's sons" (Gal. 4:4,5, "Good News for Modern Man," American Bible Society).

Paul the apostle wrote these words—to struggling Christian churches in Galatia—just a few years after Christ had died, risen from the dead and ascended into heaven. And Paul had a good reason to write like this. These brand-new Christian churches were slipping into the same mistake that too many people are making today: equating Christianity with performance, with laws and ritual.

In those very first days the church had many Jewish Christians who seemed ready to go along with the Gospel of Christ, but who believed that you had to add Jewish works and traditions as well. Some of these Judaizers had made it their business to "straighten out" some of the churches in Galatia that Paul had started—at Lydia, Antioch, Iconium, Lystra and Derbe. The Jewish Christians let the Gentile converts in these cities know that if they wanted to be *real* Christians they had to submit to the Jewish rite of circumcision, know the difference between pure and impure foods (according to Jewish law) and to keep Jewish feast days and other traditional ceremonies.

In short, there was a formidable group in the early church who believed that Christianity was nothing more than a further development of Judaism and that performance was its most important product.

And so Paul took pen in hand to write to these churches to let them know that winning Brownie points by observing a list of no-no's was not exactly what Jesus Christ had in mind when He died on the cross and rose again from the dead. He tried to explain to the Galatian Christians that before Christ came, *all* people, Jews and Gentiles, were like little children. They were trying to obey laws but they had no real control or power. People knew they could not possibly fulfill the requirements of their laws and so they lived in a sense of fear, guilt and failure.

And that is why Paul says that when God was ready—according to His timetable—He sent Jesus Christ to free mankind from a life of slavery under the Law. Paul probably had two things in mind here: Jewish laws which were exact and detailed; but also, moral principles known to all men. As J. B. Phillips puts it: ". . . while we were 'children' we lived under the authority of basic moral principles" (Gal. 4:3, *The New Testament in Modern English*).

Paul reminds the Galatians that before they knew Christ they had been slaves to their pagan gods—"gods" that did not even exist. Paul is wondering why they want to go back to becoming slaves to another poor, weak, useless religion which insists that they get to heaven by obeying laws. (See Gal. 4:8,9, *Living New Testament*.)

A relationship, not a rulebook

Paul's letter to the Galatians is typical of his

writings to Christians in the early church. Paul repeats again and again one basic idea: *To be a Christian is not a matter of obeying laws and doing good works to gain God's approval.* To be a Christian is to have a personal relationship with God. You are in God's family. You are personally related to God through your faith in Jesus Christ. That personal relationship with Christ makes you a spiritual son of God.

So, in one way, critics of Christianity such as Ringo Starr are wrong. Christians are not here to create Utopia. Christians are not here *primarily* to solve the problems of war, poverty, racial hatred and pollution. To be sure, the Christian church is supposed to be interested in all of these things because they express Christ's love in the world. But, because some Christians have "blown it" does not mean that Christianity is a second-rate superstition of some kind that is continually being pumped full of air by a tradition-bound religious establishment.

God's grace—His love and mercy—are not dependent on our ability to perform admirably or to any degree of perfection. We are saved by grace and not by works, writes Paul in Ephesians 2:8,9. But Paul goes on to say that we do good works because we know God. That is, any good works we do should come out of a gratitude to God, and because God makes us aware of needs around us.

God is not the Great Umpire in the sky

But if you make the step of belief in Christ and then fail in good works, God does not write you off. If God would write off a Christian for failure, we all would be right back in the ball game called "obey the law," and God would be the Great Umpire in the sky. God would be saying that our salvation is conditional. We would be saved *if* we performed well enough and *if* we lived up to a certain kind of standard.

If God would leave us in the dilemma of being saved *if*, it would mean that all of Christ's work, His sacrifice on the cross, His resurrection from the dead, would be meaningless. The whole point of the Gospel is that God reached down to us through Jesus Christ and did something for us that we could never do for ourselves.

But what about those good works that are supposed to come out of our belief in Christ? This is where the church seems to be sadly lacking. And this is where Ringo Starr may be partially right. Becoming a Christian does not give you a built-in reason to cop out on problems that face mankind. Becoming a Christian is supposed to make you more aware and sensitive to these problems and more eager to do something about them. When Christ came into the world it was waiting for someone who cared, for someone who could hear its screams of agony and its cries for help.

The world seems to still be waiting. The mass media—newspapers, magazines, radio and television—carry stories that picture the church as standing by, helpless or indifferent, while millions go without jobs, food, clothes, civil rights, etc. Popular music of the 1960's and 70's has a strong note of disillusionment, despair and disappointment in the establishment, especially in the church. This disappointment leads to criticism that is bitter, illogical and unfair. Ironically enough, the critics of the church are also looking for the very thing that Christ brought "in the fullness of time."

Eleanor Rigby vs. Jesus Is a Soul Man

The Beatles sing about Father McKenzie who writes sermons that no one will hear because no one comes near. And that last line of "Eleanor Rigby" ponders the fate of all those lonely people. Where do they all come from? And where do they all belong?

"Eleanor Rigby" was the Beatles' way of putting down the institutional church for failing to reach all the lonely people. John Lennon teamed up with Paul McCartney to write "Rigby," the same year that Lennon made his well-publicized remark about being more popular than Jesus. As the Beatles looked at the practically empty churches in their native England, and at many churches in America that weren't getting any fuller, they decided that Christianity had died. The doleful strains of "Eleanor Rigby" were its epitaph.

"Eleanor Rigby" is a sad song — not because the Beatles are right but because they are so wrong. You see, it's easy to criticize the institution called the church. It's easy to say, "I tried Christianity and it failed."

But there is a vast difference between "trying Christianity" and trusting Jesus Christ. There is a vast difference between joining the Christian establishment and entering into a personal relationship with Jesus Christ, the Son of God. Those who have entered into this personal relationship with Christ sing songs that are the complete reversal of "Eleanor Rigby." People with a personal relationship to Christ sing about Jesus being a soul man and how they are sold on Him.

It really does little good to sit around and chop the church because it seems to have failed. Christianity came into a world that was ready for its message. Christianity met personal needs then and it can meet personal needs today through the Person of Jesus Christ.

You can't go back and rewrite church history. There is not a great deal you can do about the so-called failure of the church. But you *can* do something about your personal commitment to Jesus Christ (just as Jim did, see p. 11).

In the following chapters you will take a look at the lives of people in the New Testament—people who responded to God through faith. They didn't join an organization. They didn't follow some "heavenly plan for success." But the lives of these people—John the Baptist, Jesus Christ, Lazarus, Mary and Martha, Peter, Stephen, Paul, Barnabas, Thomas and Timothy — all speak of the need to get your priorities straight. Christ first, everything else second. That is always the choice. It always will be.

Contrary to John Lennon's opinion, Christianity is not going to vanish or shrink. Jesus will not go away. His very name reminds you there is no neutral ground, no "cop-out country" where you can

10

Jim: "I got connected back to God"

Jim Hassmer has been a valedictorian, an outstanding tennis star, representative of his high school at Boys' State and is on the list of *Who's Who of American High School Students*. He doesn't waste time knocking the church. He's too busy really trying Jesus Christ:

"About three years ago, I got connected back to God through Jesus Christ. It doesn't take too much looking around to see that people have problems. Fears, prejudice, bickering in families, selfishness—these things are in all of us. And, no matter how hard we try, we can't completely change, not by ourselves. We have this thing called sin in us, which only God can take out. But how does he? Well, isn't this what the message of Christmas is all about? And Easter? Jesus Christ came to die, so we would be forgiven, and a new purity put inside. Linked to him, we are clean inside. We can be truly 'beautiful people.'

"Christ is someone personal, not just some abstract entity. He can be living in any person. Christ died for a purpose—to bridge the gap that had been created between us and God. Through Jesus Christ, we can come back into a relationship with God; it's like a fifth dimension.

"Christianity is reasonable—it's logical—we don't have to commit intellectual suicide to be Christians. We can love God with our minds, too. It *is* a sound philosophical system and more—it actually works to change our attitude."

—Jim Hassmer, Alexandria, Va.'

do your thing and live it up until you are old and gray and "ready for religion and all that stuff."

As you examine the profiles of faith on the following pages you will see that when it comes to God you are dealing with an ultimate paradox.

How will you handle life?

You must take your choice.

How will you handle it?

Analyze your personal attitude toward Christ and the church by checking the comment that best fits how you feel:

_____1. The church has blown it; it is hypocritical, ineffectual, and unreal.

_____2. Christianity is okay, I guess, but I don't get too much out of it. Praying and Bible reading are a drag. I wish I could be more enthusiastic, but I can't.

_____3. The institutional church may have its problems, but Jesus is a soul man and I'm sure sold on Him.

_____4. Perhaps none of the above remarks quite fits how you feel. See if you can put your feelings into one sentence. _____

If you want to "'change the church," why not start with yourself? Romans 12 is a blueprint for personal change. Read it in *The Living Bible;* then think of specific ways to let God remake you from within.

Ephesians 4 is a short course in Christian growth. Read it and think of specific steps you can take to grow into the mature person you want to be.

Above all, pray without ceasing about the criticism of the church. Much of it is unfair and unwarranted; much of it is deserved but perhaps it is God's way of waking up sincere believers who love the church and want to change it according to His will.

The teen-ager plunked himself down in a chair and addressed his pastor with a question that was gnawing at his insides: "Pastor, will I be lost and go to hell if I doubt?"

"What makes you ask that?" replied his pastor.

"The longer I sit in biology, the harder it is for me to believe the Bible. At first, I just brushed the doubts aside. I know the teacher is an agnostic and he really enjoys having roast Christian for lunch but . . ."

"And what do you think about this teacher's approach to biology and the Bible now?"

13

"I don't know. Some of the things he says make sense, and when they make sense, I begin to doubt my salvation. Pastor, I've got to know—is it a sin to doubt?"[1]

This kind of interview is repeated many times and in many ways but the basic question is always the same: "What about my doubts and is it right for me to say I'm a Christian and still have them?"

Is it really a sin to doubt?

You aren't in Christian company very long before you get the distinct impression that having doubts is not the "in thing" to do. Doubt is the very antithesis of faith. By implication, inference or direct accusation, Christians tend to let each other know that "to doubt is to sin."

And yet, Christians do have doubts. Most just don't feel free to admit it. And so they play the little game called "pious believer." To hear some people tell it in prayer meeting or testimony time, they believed in Christ and haven't had the shadow of a doubt ever since.

That's a lot of baloney and the more of it that Christians slice, the harder it is for them to handle the doubts they have tucked away deep in their hearts. Instead of using their doubts to actually help strengthen their faith, Christians keep looking for some superfaithful type who constantly oozes with enthusiasm, optimism and what appears to be unshakable belief.

Instead of grappling with doubts and learning to live with them, many Christians try to sweep them under the rug. Doubts are treated like "no-no's"—those nasty little sins we used to do before we were saved. Now that our sins are washed away we simply don't do these things anymore.

For our Scriptural proof-text to be sure that we are right in labeling doubt as one of the worst of sins, we go to James 1:6-8: "He who doubts is like a wave of the sea, blown and tossed by the wind. That man should not think he will receive anything from the Lord; he is a double-minded man, unstable in all he does" (*NIV*).

Now, there is no doubt about it: The Scriptures make it plain that being in a state of doubt is never God's will for any Christian. What James is saying here is that if we doubt and become so confused and frustrated by a lack of faith, God can't give us the wisdom and the happiness that He has for us.

What! John the Baptist a doubter???

And yet it seems that almost every believer experiences doubt at certain times. Even the giants of the faith had their weak moments. For example, John the Baptist — the last of the fearless prophets who proclaimed the coming of the Messiah — faltered at one point. Doubt hit him — and hard. Perhaps the prison cell he was in had something to do with it. Perhaps lying there, rotting in Herod's fortress, not even being able to see the sun, didn't help his faith any.

The story is found in Matthew 11 (with an important addition in Matthew 14). John, who had been born some six months before Jesus, was called to the unique task of being the forerunner of Christ. In other words, John was Jesus' press agent. He went up and down the land telling people to repent of their sins and to get ready for the coming of the Messiah.

John told the people: "With water I baptize those who repent of their sins; but Someone else is coming, far greater than I am, so great that I am not worthy to carry His shoes! He shall baptize you with the Holy Spirit and with fire" (Matt. 3:11, LNT).

And then came the day when Jesus asked John to baptize Him. John hesitated, saying that it should be the other way around, but Jesus insisted. And as they came up out of the water, God's voice was heard saying, "This is My beloved Son, and I am wonderfully pleased with Him" (Matt. 3:17, LNT). On that day, John must have been absolutely sure that Jesus was the long-awaited deliverer of Israel.

But a few months later John's fearless attitude towards sin got him into real trouble. He was in Galilee where Herod was the king. Herod had a brother—Philip—who lived in Rome with his wife. Herod also had a wife—the daughter of the king of Nabatean Arabs. But Herod had visited Rome and become acquainted with Herodias, the wife of his brother Philip. He became so well acquainted that he decided he'd rather have her instead of his own wife. He seduced Herodias away from her own husband, divorced his Arabian wife and settled down to live happily ever after in his own particular state of first century situation ethics.

16

But John the Baptist popped Herod's new-morality bubble in a hurry. He openly accused the king of divorcing his own wife without cause and committing adultery by taking away the wife of another man. To openly rebuke Herod was equal to suicide. Herod's soldiers found John and locked him up. The Bible doesn't say what John was charged with. Perhaps they called it "inciting the people to riot by telling them the truth about their king."

So John found himself in a dungeon in Herod's fortress prison—Marchaerus—high in the mountains near the Dead Sea. Why didn't Herod just put John to death and be done with it? Herod was too cunning for that. He knew that John was popular with the people and to kill him would be more than the people would take at that time. Besides, while he disliked John's criticism of him, Herod was fascinated by this wild and rough character from the desert who seemed to speak for God Himself (see Mark 6:20, *LNT*).

And so the days went by and John the Baptist—the lion who had always roamed free in the desert—became a house cat chained in an underground dungeon.

Eventually the doubts about Christ started to come. John knew the Jewish teachings about the Messiah as well as any man. And quite likely John held the view that the Messiah would come with power to renew Israel and release her from political bondage. Because of his emphasis on repentance of sin, John was probably particularly impressed by Old Testament prophecies saying the

Messiah would come in judgment of sin. (See Isa. 35:5; 61:3 for examples.)

But reports began to filter in to John through the prison grapevine (and possibly friends occasionally got to visit him). The reports told about how Jesus seemed to be bothering with a lot of unimportant things—widows, lepers, blind beggars, etc. All this was good, of course, but what about the real task at hand—establishing God's kingdom and doing something about the Roman oppressors who held Israel captive?

Had John been wrong when he called Christ the Lamb of God back there at the riverbank? Was John wrong in believing that Jesus was the Messiah promised in Scripture? Was Jesus really trying to set the people free? The roars of the desert lion were stilled and now he could only whimper and wonder if his faith in Jesus was worth it all.

So here we have John, and he is the picture of the man described in James 1:6-8. He is tossed to and fro on the waves of doubt. He seems to be double-minded about Jesus. What should he do?

Consider the possibilities: He could cop out— that is, apologize to Herod and return quietly to preaching a somewhat more diplomatic kind of message. True, it would mean compromise, but it also would mean freedom. And for a man who had spent years in the wide open spaces that dungeon was growing smaller every day.

On the other hand, he might try to make a deal with Herod. Apply a little situation ethics, perhaps. Explain to Herod that he had probably done "the loving thing" by marrying Philip's wife. After all, it would have been hypocritical for the two of them to have loved one another and gone on living with their own spouses. This too would be a cop-out, but it would be a way of saving face.

Of course, John could always grit his teeth and decide to simply sit it out. Resign himself to his fate and simply not ask questions. This is the old humble pie, "I'm spiritual, and whatever is God's will for me I will accept it with no questions asked" approach.

But Matthew 11 tells us that John didn't do any of these. To cop out or make a deal with Herod would be unthinkable for a man with John's convictions about sin. To sit quietly and let doubts fester and grow was not John's nature either. From John you can learn that there are two kinds of doubt: *positive* and *negative*.

Are your doubts positive or negative?

If John had chosen an attitude of negative doubt he would have simply "sat it out," doing nothing. To doubt negatively is to do nothing about your doubts and let them slowly, almost imperceptibly, turn into unbelief.

Negative doubt slowly but surely quenches any fires of faith that you might have. A lot of people carry a big load of negative doubt. They simply go along and act as if they are as spiritual and as faithful as the next guy. They don't dare tell anybody how they really feel. They don't dare ask the dreaded questions that would expose their doubts to others—especially other believers. And of course, they wouldn't dare admit to someone such as the pastor that they have doubts—that, for example, they can't quite buy every point of doctrine in the Christian faith.

But John didn't stay trapped under a load of negative doubt. He sent some of his own followers to Jesus and asked one question: "Are you really the one we are looking for, or shall we keep on looking?" When he asked that question John exercised the power of *positive* doubting. He took his doubt to the only One who could really give him any answers.

Positive doubt can lead to deeper faith. Negative doubt will inevitably lead to unbelief. It is not a sin to doubt or to have doubts creep into your mind. But unless you do something about the doubts they can subtly turn into unbelief and that *is* sin.

Unbelief is not a sin because it is some extra naughty "no-no." Unbelief is an attitude that automatically puts you at odds with God Himself. And that is exactly what sin is: to be at odds with God, to choose to not believe him, to be in rebellion against him actively or passively.

Descartes, the sixteenth century skeptic-philosopher said: "I doubt that I may know." The Christian takes Descartes' skepticism one step further and says, "I doubt that I may *grow*."

And growth is often painful. To be willing to do something about your doubts doesn't automatically sweep them away. The power of positive doubting doesn't always result in a nice, neat, happy ending. John the Baptist would be the first to admit it.

When John sent his two disciples to talk to Jesus

FAITH

DOUBT

Matthew 11:3

and ask Him if He were really the Messiah or
should they look for someone else, what was Jesus'
answer? Did He give John a careful, gentle explanation and a pat on the back? Did He send him encouragement with a "thinking of you" card?

Not exactly.

Jesus told John's disciples, "Go back to John and
tell him about the miracles you've seen Me do—the
blind people I've healed, and the lame people now
walking without help, and the cured lepers, and
the deaf who hear, and the dead raised to life; and
tell him about My preaching the Good News to the
poor. Then give him this message, 'Blessed are
those who don't doubt Me'" (Matt. 11:4-6, LNT).

And so back went John's disciples with that message. No pardon from the dungeon. No gentle
words of reassurance or encouragement. But something else—something possibly even more valuable.
In His inimitable way, Jesus gave John something
really useful.

But what did John say? How did he take this
rather "short answer" sent back to him from Jesus?

We don't know because Scripture doesn't really
say, but suppose—just suppose—things might have
gone something like this:

Let's call the two disciples that John sent to
Jesus *Seth* and *Hillel*. Back to the dungeon come
Seth and Hillel, and John eagerly asks them what
they have learned from Christ. With perplexity and
no little hesitation, they tell John what Jesus said.
But John does not throw himself on the dungeon
floor in despair. He doesn't gnaw at the bars in futile rage. He simply says: "Jesus turns us back to

22

the Scriptures to find Him — these are the words Isaiah used as he prophesied concerning the Christ. The voice of the Scriptures and the voice of Jesus of Nazareth are one voice."

But Seth and Hillel aren't quite so sure. What about the fiery judgment in the prophetic writings?

John has an answer for that. "We have not grasped the order of the divine plan. Go to the Scriptures and study them again. There are many things I don't understand either. I must give myself to prayer. But I know that God has answered. Jesus of Nazareth is indeed the Lamb of God who fulfills the words of the prophets."

Now this is only a fictional idea of what may have happened.[3] But who is to say that John did not say something just about like this? Not that John had all the answers. He still had plenty of questions. But somehow he knew that Jesus spoke the truth — that Jesus was the Christ and the only possible answer.

Not long after, Herod tired of his little game and he let himself be tricked into promising Salome, the daughter of his wife, anything she wanted. According to her mother's wishes she wanted John's head, and she got it on a silver platter. (See Matt. 14:1-12.)

Not much of a happy ending here. At least, not as far as earthly things are concerned. We are disappointed. We always like to have a "happy ending." We want all the answers to be pleasant. But the faith that always looks for all the answers and happy endings is not the faith that is hammered out of the real stuff of life. Wanting all the answers

and happy endings is a phony "cotton candy" kind
of faith that melts away when the first storm
comes.

To have doubts is to be human

When it comes to talking about doubts, every
Christian should get one thing straight: It is no sin
to have them. It is no sin to get concerned when
unbelievers lay it on you with their theories of evo-
lution and how science and the Bible don't seem to
match up. It is no sin for the Christian to ask these
questions on his own. To have doubts is to admit
that you are human, finite. Anyone who claims that
he's never had any doubts is claiming that he has
perfect knowledge, that he has a hot-line to the in-
finite mind of God. Few people run around claiming this. At least they don't run around loose.

For most of us doubts are inescapable. It's not a
question of, "Do I have any doubts?" The question
is, "Do I doubt *positively* or *negatively?*" Am I
willing to bring my doubts out into the open spaces
of my mind and confront them honestly with the
promises in Scripture? (See Jann's testimony, p.
25.)

It helps to remember that even Jesus had doubts.
Doubt after all is a special form of temptation, and
wasn't Jesus tempted in every way that we are, yet
without sin? (See Heb. 4:15.)[4] The human side of
our Lord must have had its moments of uncertainty
there in the wilderness or the devil would have
never made his entrance.

And what about Christ's agony in the Garden of

Jann: "The first few days are the hardest . . ."

"The first few days after meeting Christ are some of the hardest. Your old nature, your old routine, has had control and wants to put every doubt it can muster into your mind: 'It isn't real, I don't feel any different than before, forget it, it was all a hoax.'

"But God promises that once we accept Him, we're in His Family. The Bible says, 'Some, however, did receive him (Christ) and believed in him; so he gave them the right to become God's children' (John 1:12, "Good News for Modern Man"). When we blow it, that certainly doesn't kick us out of the family! True, it does break down communication between us and our Father, but it doesn't change our relationship.

"God's love is unconditional, unchanging. If we hold on to bad habits built up over the last sixteen (or whatever) years, or yield to new temptations, we simply admit it and get it out into the open with God. The Bible explains, 'If we freely admit that we have sinned, we find God utterly reliable and straightforward—he forgives our sins and makes us thoroughly clean from all that is evil' (1 John 1:9, *The New Testament in Modern English*).

"For awhile, I was sort of living half and half—one day with Jesus, the next day in my own way, what I felt like doing. And it was terribly frustrating. I finally said, 'I'm sick of this; I want Jesus to control all of my life.' In this way, I've found peace. The more we believe, the more we walk with Christ."

—Jann Reynolds, San Diego, Calif.[3]

Gethsemane? Could it be that the man Jesus had His moments of uncertainty and doubt, but that they were offset by His unconquerable faith in His Heavenly Father?[6]

Don't be afraid of doubts. Go ahead and admit you have a few questions, a few uncertainties. Or, maybe you are like the boy who needed to come right out with it and tell his dad, "I don't believe in God anymore." His father, who was a college professor, might have gone into a long lecture on the existence of God and why it is foolish for anyone to say he doesn't believe in Him. But the father was too wise for that. He simply said, "That's all right, son. God still believes in you."[7]

You see, God can be positive about your doubts. He can still believe in you. So what is your choice?

You can have negative doubts and possibly wind up not believing in Him.

Or, you can use the power of positive doubting and it will help you believe in Him all the more!

How will you handle it?

Want to practice the power of positive doubting? Here are some steps you can take:

1. Don't act like the doubts aren't there. Admit them to yourself and realize that God knows, too.

"O Lord, you have examined my heart and know everything about me. You know when I sit or stand. When far away you know my every thought. You chart the path ahead of me, and tell me where to stop and rest. Every moment, you know where I am." (Ps. 139:1-3, *TLB*).

* * * * * *

26

2. Once you admit you have doubts or questions or uncertainties, rejoice in the fact that the Bible teaches that God accepts you and your doubts and will not turn His back on you.

"Come to Me and I will give you rest—all of you who work so hard beneath a heavy yoke. Wear My yoke—for it fits perfectly—and let Me teach you; for I am gentle and humble, and you shall find rest for your souls; for I give you only light burdens" (Matt. 11:28-30, *LNT*).

"Let Him have all your worries and cares, for He is always thinking about you and watching everything that concerns you" (1 Pet. 5:7, *LNT*).

* * * * * *

3. Study the Scriptures (even if you aren't sure you believe them). Since it is God you are doubting, why not go to His Book and get His side of it? Try to be an informed doubter, not an ignorant one. It might be that when you see what the Bible actually has to say on some things your doubts won't be there any longer.

"But the people of Beroea were more open-minded than those in Thessalonica, and gladly listened to the message. They searched the Scriptures day by day to check up on Paul and Silas' statements to see if they were really so" (Acts 17:11, *LNT*).

"You search the Scriptures, for you believe they give you eternal life. And the Scriptures point to Me!" (John 5:39, *LNT*).

* * * * * *

4. Ask questions. Talk to people you feel you can trust and who will accept you and your questions. They may be able to give you some help or perhaps you will feel you are helping them because you have freed them to admit that they have a few questions too.

"Share each other's troubles and problems, and so obey our Lord's command" (Gal. 6:2, *LNT*).

* * * * * *

5. Be sure to do plenty of praying and thinking of

your own—on your own. Christianity is, after all, a personal relationship to Jesus Christ. Share your life with Christ. Share your doubts too, and see what happens.

"But when you pray, go away by yourself, all alone, and shut the door behind you and pray . . ." (Matt. 6:6, LNT).

"Ask, and you will be given what you ask for. Seek, and you will find. Knock, and the door will be opened" (Matt. 7:7, LNT).

* * * * * *

6. If there is something that you can actually do—some action to take—do it. If you have feelings of guilt and can't get rid of them, ask God to take them away. That is, after all, His specialty.

"You haven't tried this before, [but begin now]. Ask, using My name, and you will receive, and your cup of joy will overflow" (John 16:24, LNT).

* * * * * *

7. Keep in mind that to "doubt positively" is not to go around looking for more doubts because you think this is a way to grow in your faith. Few people have to look for more doubts; enough of them arrive on their own. If doubt isn't a big problem for you thank God for your certainty and ask Him to keep your faith strong for those days when doubts may come.

"For I know the one in whom I trust, and I am sure that He is able to safely guard all that I have given Him until the day of His return" (2 Tim. 1:12, LNT).

"For I am convinced that nothing can ever separate us from His love. Death can't, and life can't. . . . Our fears for today, our worries about tomorrow . . . nothing will ever be able to separate us from the love of God demonstrated by our Lord Jesus Christ when He died for us" (Rom. 8:38, 39, LNT).

"This certain hope of being saved is a strong and trustworthy anchor for our souls, connecting us with God Himself behind the sacred curtains of heaven" (Heb. 6:19, LNT).

IT TAKES MORE THAN BREAD...

What does the word "temptation" mean to you?

According to Webster, to tempt means to "entice to do wrong by promise of pleasure or gain."

"Pleasure or gain. . . ." That's not bad. That's pretty close. No matter how we define temptation there's always that element of pleasure or gain and along with it, that little warning light or bell of conscience that tells us "maybe you shouldn't."

For example, you're on the way home in your new Hugger. It's late. No traffic. The car's so new you haven't had a chance yet to see what it will really do. . . .

You're baby-sitting for a couple who see you as a sensible, trustworthy girl. They've been gone about half an hour. You've just wrestled the kids into bed.

The phone rings. It's Johnny and he wants to come over. But the rule is, "No boys in the house. . . ."

You've stuck to your diet for two and a half days. This time you're determined to lose those ugly ten pounds. Then along comes a friend with a bag of your favorite goodies and of course she offers you some. Well, why not? What's the harm in eating just one. . . .

All of us face temptation. On the Christian scene it seems that it gets faced more often. At least Christians are more aware of temptation (or talk like they are). Christians even pray, "Lead us not into temptation but deliver us from evil." And that's just the catch—how do you get delivered from evil? The answer is right in the Lord's Prayer itself. Jesus taught it to His disciples to help them commit themselves to God and to rely on Him for power when they were tempted. Jesus Himself did this when He was tempted.

Yes, Jesus knew temptation. It's true He had power far beyond mere mortal men—power to heal, power to alter natural law. But Hebrews 4:15 tells us that Jesus ". . . understands our weaknesses, since He had the same temptations we do . . ." (*LNT*).

How do we know Jesus faced all the temptations we face? Matthew and Luke tell it like it was. Jesus had just been baptized by John at the River Jordan. The Holy Spirit had descended upon Him and God had said, "This is my beloved Son in whom I am well pleased" (Matt. 3:17). It was a high point of Jesus' life—the beginning of His public ministry and the promise of a bright career lay ahead. But first, there would be the final exams....

"Then Jesus, full of the Holy Spirit, left the Jordan River, being urged by the Spirit out into the barren wastelands of Judea, where Satan tempted Him for forty days. He ate nothing all that time, and was very hungry" (Luke 4:1, *LNT*).

And so Jesus went from the glory of the Jordan baptism to the barren wastes of the Judean desert. There is no spot on earth more barren, no more "Godforsaken." The sun bakes the dust and the rocks like a blowtorch. The daytime temperatures often soar above 140 degrees. It was here that Jesus was led by the Spirit to think things over. And it was here that Satan tempted Him in the three basic ways that he tempts all of us.

As you watch Jesus face these three great temptations, keep a key point in mind: *Jesus is being tempted to use His great power in a way that will cause Him to compromise in one way or another.* Compromise is often the first step in yielding to temptation.

First Satan said, "If you are God's Son, tell this stone to become a loaf of bread" (Luke 4:3, *LNT*).

In a way, this first temptation seems reasonable enough. Fasting makes you hungry and when you're hungry it's logical to stop and have a bite to eat. But the point is, the Holy Spirit had led Jesus into the desert and part of that leading was that He would take no food. If Jesus broke His fast it would mean gratifying His physical appetite instead of doing what God had led Him to do.

In a very innocent and seemingly reasonable way (which is typical of Satan) Jesus was tempted to

31

rebel against God by satisfying physical desires.

Now, while we aren't tempted to turn stones into bread, we are certainly tempted daily—even hourly —to go against God in order to satisfy physical desire. The appetites that God built into us bring us much pleasure. They can also bring us much grief and despair. It is an ironic rule—a sort of moral law of physics—that we can oversatisfy physical appetite to our own destruction.

The 1960's and 70's have brought a revolution of change crashing down on the entire world. Out of this revolution has come the most incredible bombardment of the physical senses (appetites) ever known. Today you don't have to fast in the desert to be tempted. Just turn on the television set. Just walk down the street. Flip open any number of magazines, newspapers and other beautifully illustrated full-color materials and you will find stories, pictures, slogans, all carefully calculated to "give you an appetite" of one kind or another.

Playboy: sick sex via the centerfold

Obviously, the most overworked item is sex. It almost seems that sex is the great high god and teachers of the new morality are its prophets. But it's not sex that is really god to many people. What they actually worship is pleasure—and sex is only one way of obtaining what they think is pleasure.

Playboy magazine and similar publications are well known for their emphasis on sex. *Playboy* peddles an immature and sick point of view that basically urges its readers to love things and use people (especially well-endowed women). After more than sixteen years it is still that center fold that sells *Playboy*; *not* what it advertises as sophisticated interviews, "high-class" fiction, and searching analyses of society's ills.

But *Playboy* is more than sex, its point of view says "enjoy, enjoy," and each issue includes features on food, clothes, sports cars and every other material item imaginable which can bring pleasure to the physical senses. *Playboy* is a major piece of propaganda for that popular corruption of ethics called "the new morality."

The new morality has a very old line

The new morality purrs, "You've been inhibited too long. Your parents, and their parents before them, sold you a Victorian, puritanical bill of goods. They tried to make sex a no-no and they lived like a bunch of hypocrites in the process. But now you're free. You can create meaningful relationships right out in the open with no hypocrisy. Just do your own thing. As long as nobody gets hurt, pleasure is the goal and there's no limit."

When seen in the light of the blinking neons of the new morality, Satan's tempting little question, "Why don't you turn these stones into bread?" doesn't seem quite so tame. All the elements are there and all Jesus has to do is give in to a normal, healthy physical appetite. After all, He's just about starved, isn't He? But Jesus doesn't give in. He says, "Man shall not live by bread alone" (Luke 4:4). The account of Matthew adds, ". . . but by

33

every word that proceedeth out of the mouth of God" (Matt. 4:4).

Comedians, cartoonists and politicians, to name a few, like to take Jesus' "not by bread alone" statement and use it to gain laughs, votes, etc., but its truth is undeniable. Life is more than satisfying physical appetites. If all you live for is food, drink, sex or other sensual enjoyments, sooner or later you get that overstuffed feeling. You get bored. Man can't live by bread (pleasure) alone because man is not built that way. He is programmed with a desire to know his Creator, to love Him and be loved in return.

But ever since Adam we've been lousing it up. We turn from the Creator to things, to material and physical pleasures. We think this is where it's at, and when we get there, we find that we are nowhere.

There is no better example of thinking that pleasure is "where it's at" and winding up nowhere than drug abuse. But as many a doper knows, the stakes are high when you play games with drugs. You like to think you can get away with it, but the odds are against you and if you play long enough you can go clear to the bottom.

The following "Paraphrase of the Twenty-Third Psalm" was found in a Long Beach, California, phone booth by a police officer. It was written by a 20-year-old heroin addict who was trying to kick his habit. For added impact and comparison, the Biblical version of what many call the most beautiful psalm in Scripture appears in roman type with the doper's version immediately following in italics:

34

The LORD is my shepherd; I shall not want.
King heroin is my shepherd, I shall always want.
He maketh me to lie down in green pastures:
He maketh me to lie down in the gutters:
He leadeth me beside the still waters.
He leadeth me beside the troubled waters.
He restoreth my soul:
He destroyeth my soul.
He leadeth me in the path of righteousness
for his name's sake.
He leadeth me in the path of wickedness
for effort's sake.
Yea, though I walk through the valley of the shadow
of death, I will fear no evil:
Yea, I shall walk through the valley of poverty and
will fear all evil:
For thou art with me;
For thou, heroin, art with me;
Thy rod and thy staff they comfort me.
Thy needle and capsule try to comfort me.
Thou preparest a table before me in the presence
of mine enemies:
Thou strippest the table of groceries in the presence
of my family:
Thou anointest my head with oil; my cup runneth over.
Thou robbest my head of reason, my cup of sorrow
runneth over.
Surely goodness and mercy shall follow me all the
days of my life: and I will dwell in the house of
the LORD forever.
Surely, heroin addiction shall stalk me all the
days of my life and I will dwell in the house of
the damned forever.

The junkie wrote a potent paraphrase to say the least, but maybe you think it sounds like a scare tactic. Many a doper and most "straights" would reply by saying, "It'll never happen to me."

Maybe it won't, but drugs are only one way to put "bread" ahead of God—especially in an affluent, materialistic society. If a lot of people—Christians among them—would be honest, their own paraphrase of the twenty-third psalm would read: "Money, cars, clothes, popularity, television, fun and games, or just plain kicks are *my* shepherd and I just can't seem to get enough."

Is the pursuit of happiness out of control?

America's forefathers put a beautiful idea into writing when they said: "All men are created equal and are endowed by their Creator with certain inalienable rights, among these, life, liberty and the pursuit of happiness." But that pursuit of happiness has turned into a pursuit of pleasure and a lot of people are out of control. They have fallen into the ancient trap called hedonism—the literal worship of pleasure—making pleasure and comfort and self-indulgence the most important things in life.

The worship of pleasure and the worship of God do not mix. Inevitably, you shove God into the background and "put your belly on the altar of worship." Again and again the Bible issues grim warnings against selfishness and self-indulgence. Paul realized there were plenty of hedonists who tried to claim loyalty to Christ:

When writing to his good friend and protégé

Timothy, Paul warned, ". . . in the last days it is going to be very difficult to be a Christian.

"For people will love only themselves and their money; they will be proud and boastful, sneering at God, disobedient to their parents, ungrateful to them, and thoroughly bad.

"They will be hardheaded and never give in to others; they will be constant liars and trouble-makers and will think nothing of immorality. They will be rough and cruel, and sneer at those who try to be good.

"They will betray their friends; they will be hot-headed, puffed up with pride, and prefer good times to worshiping God" (2 Tim. 3:1-4).

Preferring good times to worshiping God. . . . That is the real issue. That is the very real temptation that faces anyone who is living in the affluence and technology of the space age. But while scientific advancements have done a lot for our bodies (just think of medical achievements as one example), there is a question about what technology has done for our souls.

Where do you find your pleasure?

The Bible promises pleasure, but it is pleasure of another kind. The Scriptures teach that real satisfaction doesn't come from filling your stomach with gourmet food, your closet with the latest fashions and your garage with Detroit's finest hardware. *Real satisfaction comes from a relationship to God that has you depending on Him,* not things for joy and fulfillment.

37

There are different ways to seek pleasure in life. A popular approach is to associate pleasure with human appetites—kicks. Pleasure is found in possessions, material objects, good food, sex, and as one airline ad put it, "unwinding in Tahiti tomorrow." The other way to seek pleasure is to turn yourself over to God. God has provided the way and the means in Jesus Christ. Jesus said that He had come to give life and life more abundantly (John 10:10).

And what is an abundant life? Psychologists give various lists of what all human beings need. Two basic psychological needs in all of us are love and a feeling of self-worth. If you can't feel that somebody, somewhere, really loves you, with no strings attached, you will not be happy. And right along with that, if you can't feel that you are worth something to someone, somewhere, and that you really matter to somebody or some group, you will not find real pleasure in life.

To feel that you are loved and that you are worth something is to feel that your life counts, that you are able to accomplish something worthwhile. The Bible calls this "fruitfulness." The key to pleasure for every Christian is found in John 15:5. Jesus is talking to His disciples on the night before His crucifixion. He is drawing an analogy concerning vines and fruit. He compares Himself to the vine and His disciples to the branches of that vine: "It is the man who shares my life and whose life I share who proves fruitful. For the plain fact is that apart from me you can do nothing

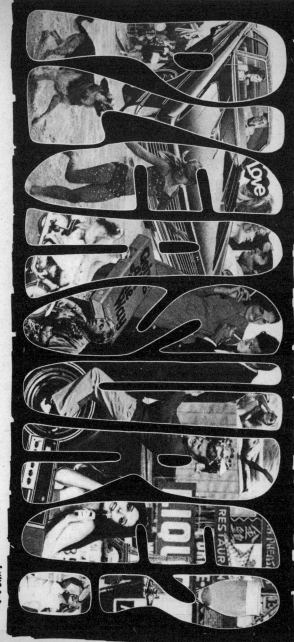

LUKE 4:4

. . ." (John 15:5, *The New Testament in Modern English*).

Any Christian can trace real and lasting pleasure, which comes from God, right back to his obedience to Christ and his willingness to share his life with Christ. And any Christian can trace a lack of pleasure in his Christian life—frustration, bitterness, disillusionment—right back to disobedience to Christ and an unwillingness to truly share his life with his Lord.

The Christian life is a beautiful thing. God reaches down to do something for a person which that person cannot do for himself. All Christians are saved from the penalty of sin and the power of sin over their lives because of God's mercy and favor. But then God doesn't push the Christian around. He doesn't move in and say, "Now that I've saved you, I'm going to run your life my way." He still respects every person's free will and right to choose. He does not legislate love, but He lets it develop and grow in each Christian as that Christian allows it to grow.

And it follows that God doesn't bring "automatic and instant pleasure" to the Christian on a continual basis. When a person believes in Christ, God doesn't put him in overdrive and on a continual "high" that never goes away. There is trusting and depending and believing to do. This kind of trusting and believing has nothing to do with working your way to heaven, but it is a response that involves your will. Christ doesn't ask you to earn your way but He does say, "Yield yourself to My Holy Spirit. Trust Me, relate to Me."

Chris: "My goal was to get the most for the least . . ."

"My constant goal was to get the most out of life by putting the least into it—no matter who was stepped on. Everything was relative; material objects obsessed me. Money was my god. Still, since those were the very principles on which society operated, I considered myself to be a pretty decent guy.

"So when someone on campus mentioned Jesus, I immediately questioned His practicality. Fourteen years of Sunday school had been bad news. Yet I realized soon that this was not even the issue. Rather, the issue was allowing Christ to 'flesh out' His life through me, smooth out the rough spots and empower me. . . .

"First, I saw that through Christ my life was no longer enslaved to natural circumstance—what will come, will come, etc. As Christ opened up my horizon, I could think of others unselfishly. I escaped from being the problem to becoming part of the solution. I agree with many of the radical groups that the world needs to be changed, but through Christ, not through wars. So I'm committed to a Person and to a cause worth dying for. That's living."

—Chris Xenakis, University of Illinois[1]

To yield yourself to Christ may be the hardest work you ever do. The reason it's so hard is because you can't turn it into an ego trip. (For more on ego trips, see chapter 5.) You can't take any credit for what God's Spirit is doing in you. God will be ". . . at work within you, helping you want to obey Him, and then helping you do what He wants" (Phil. 2:13, *LNT*).

The choice is clear. Temptation is always there. You can try to go through life as Christ did (see p. 41), trying to get the most out of it by putting the least into it—and that's hedonism. That's the worship of pleasure. That's being concerned with comfort rather than commitment.

Or, you can go through life putting everything you have into loving God and obeying Him with no strings attached, no clause in the contract that reads: "What am I going to get out of it?" You don't believe in Christ for what you can get out of Him. Instead, you say, "Here I am Lord, I want You to get out of *me* whatever is there that can glorify You."

Does that sound too self-sacrificing, too noble? Go back one more time to what Jesus said to Satan. "You can't live by bread (physical pleasures) alone." Make that choice, and you will say with the psalmist, "You have let me experience the joys of life and the exquisite pleasures of your own eternal presence" (Ps. 16:11, *TLB*).

How will you handle it?

Think of at least three temptations that seem to be

facing you constantly. Analyze these temptations and see if you can discover reasons why these things are always tempting you.

Do you agree with theologian Helmut Thielicke, when he says, ". . . it is clear where temptation lies; it does not lurk without, but is within; it is not in front of us . . . but comes from behind and stands at our back. It is not some external Satan which stands between God and us; we ourselves stand between God and us . . . and do not we human beings know this only too well ourselves? Did not the rich young man know it (Mark 10:17-22)? In the last resort it was not his riches but he himself that stood between God and him; for he allowed himself to be possessed by riches."[2]

Check through the following thoughts. Which ones can you use to keep yourself from standing between you and God?

"But remember this—the wrong desires that come into your life aren't anything new and different. Many others have faced exactly the same problems before you. And no temptation is irresistible. You can trust God to keep the temptation from becoming so strong that you can't stand up against it, for He has promised this and will do what He says. He will show you how to escape temptation's power so that you can bear up patiently against it" (1 Cor. 10:13, *LNT*).

*　*　*　*　*　*

"This High Priest of ours understands our weaknesses, since He had the same temptations we do, though He never once gave way to them and sinned" (Heb. 4:15, *LNT*).

*　*　*　*　*　*

"Dear brothers, is your life full of difficulties and temptations? Then be happy, for when the way is rough, your patience has a chance to grow. Happy is the man who doesn't give in and do wrong when he is tempted, for afterwards he will get as his reward the crown of life that God has promised those who love Him" (James 1:2, 3, 12, *LNT*).

"Doing your own thing" isn't just an expression anymore . . .

It's a way of life.

"Born Free" didn't win academy awards because it sings about getting up at six and hoeing cotton. We like the idea of being free as the wind, free as grass growing in the field, free to follow our hearts. When you're born free, life *is* really worth living.

Trouble is, however, the establishment (i.e. "system") seems to have moved in and put limits on freedom. Signs of the limits are everywhere: "Don't speed" . . . "Keep off the grass" . . . "Restricted area" . . . "No running in the halls" . . . "No Smoking" . . . "Be on time" . . . "Persons with long hair must wear bathing caps". . . .

The list of rules and no-no's goes on and on. The

result is a society that is uptight. "Power Play" was a popular song that attacked authority figures and possibly the concept of authority itself. The song asks how anyone has the right to tell anyone else what to do. Who has given anyone the power to "stop me from living like I do"?

Several years ago a new TV show ("Then Came Bronson") was based on a simple plot. A young newspaper reporter got fed up with a cold, crass establishment and decided to cut out on his motorcycle to see the country and to find out who he really was. Although popular with many young people, "Then Came Bronson" died before the end of its first season, a victim of another establishment standard—the Nielson ratings.

But in its own way, "Then Came Bronson" had plenty to say about freedom. It's no accident that the directors of the show left in plenty of footage showing Bronson (actor Michael Parks) zipping along highways, climbing hills, sailing over sand dunes on his custom-made motorcycle. You got that "born free" feeling right there in front of your own tube. You were *there* . . . with Bronson . . . hair flying in the wind . . . sun dancing on your highly polished handlebars . . . bugs spattering on your carefree grin. . . .

Wanting the freedom to do their own thing is practically an obsession with many people today. For these people it seems that no matter where they turn, some authority—a parent, a teacher, a traffic cop, a pastor, a congressman, a President—is laying it on them, curbing their freedom. One thing to keep in mind is that all of us—deep inside—

want to "be in authority." When you hear somebody complaining, "They won't let me do my own
thing," he is really saying that he wants power . . .
control. This desire for power—for feeling that you
are captain of your own soul—is basic. And with
this basic desire comes a basic temptation to want
too much power.

You can want so much control over your own life
and destiny (and possibly the lives of others) that
you decide to answer to no one but yourself. You
shove God neatly aside, giving him lip service at
best. Or, perhaps you rebel openly and see God as
the ultimate authority figure running the freedom-
stifling authoritarian establishment.

The temptation to want too much power is so
basic it is no wonder that Satan used it on Christ in
the wilderness. After seeing that he wasn't getting
anywhere with his suggestion to put pleasure (turn
the stones into bread) ahead of God, Satan shifted
his approach: "Then Satan took Him up and revealed to Him all the kingdoms of the world in a
moment of time; and the Devil told Him, 'I will
give you all these splendid kingdoms and their
glory—for they are mine to give to anyone I wish—
if You will only get down on Your knees and worship me'" (Luke 4:5-7, *LNT*).

We all want to be in charge

Satan was tempting Jesus with nothing less than
sheer power. We all face this universal temptation.
Granted, no one (so far) has been offered the entire world. Few of us have a chance to rule

even one kingdom. But all of us still seek power. We want to control our own particular situation— in the family, in the peer group, at school, at church. All of us want to be able to not only get along with people but to get people to do what we want them to do.

There is an entire publishing industry that is devoted to this basic desire of wanting to control others. If you get on their mailing list, you will receive letter after letter offering you books, pamphlets, recordings, etc., that can teach you how to "win astounding control over people and events; attract to yourself money, material things, people and conditions that you wish to have in your life!"

The promotional pitch selling a book about metaphysics and dimensions of your mind tells you how you can make your "astral body" (an accumulation of your sense of sight, hearing, taste, touch and smell) materialize in front of other people at a distance.

There are other books that teach you the laws of mental domination. "Psychic masters of the mystic East" will share their secrets of how to cast an evil eye on people, how to do black magic, how to look on desired members of the opposite sex in a way that makes them "want to meet you."

That there is a market for this kind of reading is only one symptom of a natural human desire for power which becomes the prey of exploiters.

Why the revival in astrology?

Another example is astrology, which has enjoyed

a new surge of popularity in the 1960's and 70's. The musical, *Hair*, features the hit tune "The Age of Aquarius." The age of Aquarius is a 2,000 year period that supposedly began in 1904 and is to be a time when human welfare will be the prime consideration in all the world.

For some people, astrology is a kick, a fad— something to think about but not really believe in, something to use as an escape from ulcer-raising headlines describing war, murder, riots, pollution, etc. But for other people astrology is no joke. They take it quite seriously and they actually believe that the stars and planets control and affect their lives.

An experienced astrologer can make his prognostications sound quite scientific and professional. After all, to do a thorough job on you he needs the very hour and date of your birth. When he goes into seeing if you were born in the first, second or third "descan" of your zodiacal period, and what planets can influence you because of the descan you are in, it all starts sounding very impressive indeed.

But even when all the descans and planets are in place, astrology usually winds up centering on physical desires and materialism. High priority is often placed on sex and success of one kind or another.

Astrology is hotly defended by its fans and followers. They say astrology is misunderstood. Astrology is misquoted. But when all the horoscopes are cast, astrology is another attempt to grab that big brass ring called power and control. Astrology, stripped of all the flowery phrases and syrupy soliloquys, is humanistic and man-centered.

The stars and planets whirling through space millions of light years away are supposed to control your destiny and "knowing" what those stars say is a form of power. Who needs the Jehovah God? Astrology has twelve "gods"—Capricorn, Taurus, Aries, Gemini, Cancer, Leo, Virgo, Libra, Scorpio, Sagittarius, Aquarius and Pisces. Under which sign of the Zodiac were you born? Once you know, you should "worship" accordingly. You don't need the Bible. Your horoscope will tell you all. The God of the Bible doesn't have to make the scene. He isn't needed.

But if God doesn't make the scene, the scene's not complete. If you want to know what the Scriptures say about astrologers, fortune-tellers and witches, check Deuteronomy 17:2-5 and Isaiah 47:13,14. For the classic example of how a man who started out as God's servant turned from God to reliance on advice of a witch, read the sad story of King Saul in 1 Samuel 28. Keep in mind, however, that King Saul was a desperate man. Things were out of control. He was losing his grip. In a word, he pressed the panic button.

It's not a coincidence that astrology flourished in the 1920's, a period of troubled change and upheaval—and here we are again in the 1970's and 80's, the most incredible time of chaotic change in the history of the world. No wonder people desperately grasp for power of any kind.

And as they grasp for power and control they take it at any price no matter how phony they know that "power" really is. They worship anything and anyone in the deluded hope that they can feel "secure" (see Coni's story of witchcraft, p. 51).

Who do I really worship?

Isn't that the real question when it comes to being tempted to want too much power and control? If not, why did Jesus answer Satan's invitation to have power and authority over all the kingdoms of the world by telling the devil that it is written, "We must worship God, and Him alone" (Luke 4:8, *LNT*)?

Once again, Jesus says it all in less than ten words. The answer to the temptation to want too much power does not lie in debating on how much power or what kind of power. The question is: Who are you worshiping? What idol or idols are in your life because of your need to have power—to be in charge, to feel you can do your own thing?

We all long to do our own thing. And that's why offers of power and authority—even small, insignificant ones—are loaded with hang-ups.

It's all too easy to call ourselves Christians but to worship someone or something else instead of God. Perhaps that is why there seems to be a universal malady affecting Christians. We might call it "halfwayism." We want Christ as our Saviour. We like to have Him play celestial lifeguard and to know He'll get us safely across those troubled waters to the heavenly shore.

But we're not quite so sure about wanting Him

Coni: "It was smooth to feel Satan's power . . ."

"My involvement in a witch thing came partly as a result of trying to get off drugs . . . I already believed in supernatural forces, and Satan seemed like a powerful being to me.

"The dude I was living with knew a witch who had been into it for a long time. She was enthusiastic about my background—felt I could become a 'familiar' under her. Since she was responsible to Elji, a demon of destruction, she was going to teach me to destroy. . . .

". . . My job was to literally blow people's minds. My witch taught me to hurt people deliberately. I succeeded with one guy . . . —he's still in a mental hospital.

". . . My witch had me as a favorite. . . . She laid on me lots of subtle ways to get to people's heads. It was smooth to feel Satan's power.

"Then, suddenly one morning, everything in my head flashed back to the beautiful people I had known in high school and college. Why was I now trying to destroy people? Suddenly Satan's power was something I hated. This wasn't it. I took to heroin, a new drug for me, and began riding with the Gypsy Jokers. What I dug about them was their beating up people, raping girls. There lingered a sense of being under Satan's power. I was sort of a back-slid demon.

"It was an old high school friend and her husband who caught me off-guard. They told me I didn't have to look all my life for new ways to get power. They said God had a much better life for me if I would just take it. The thought of Christianity turned me off, but they shared with me their personal experience with the Person. Jesus Christ wasn't distant and inaccessible like I thought . . . eventually I asked Jesus to come into my life.

"I felt a new inner strength which enabled me to face life in a way I never had before. God was healing my mind . . . I still have a long way to go."

—Coni, Berkeley, California[1]

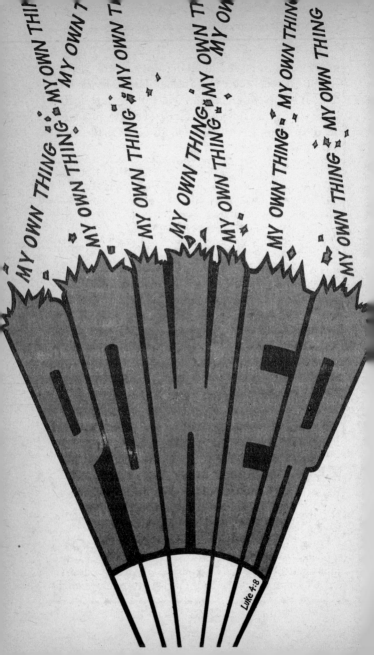

to be Lord, to be the final authority in life. Letting Christ become Lord takes time. That takes a little thinking—a little giving up. Most of us have lots of idols and it takes more than one decision, one week at camp or one spiritual crisis to clean them out of our lives.

But God is patient. Somehow He knew we'd have the problem. He didn't save us on the condition that we would "shape up" overnight or clean out every last idol in twenty-four hours. Not that He winks at our idols. Not that He's happy with us when we stamp our feet like little kids and whine that we want to do our own thing.

Instead He says, "Look! I have been standing at the door and I am constantly knocking. If anyone hears Me calling him and opens the door, I will come in and fellowship with him and he with Me" (Rev. 3:20, LNT).

Fellowship with Him or doing your own thing without Him. It depends on who you want to put in charge.

God or Satan?

Now, there *is* a choice! What will you do?

How will you handle it?

How many idols are in your life? That is, what kinds of power do you really want—and badly? Does the following paragraph give you any clues?

"Lord, I want to belong. Bill says, 'Get a car.' Fran tells me, 'Win a letter.' My dad says, 'Study harder.' John shouts, 'Raise hell!' Kay asks, 'Why not go steady?' I don't know which one is right. All those things might

53

work, I guess. Still, each in its own way, Lord, is a trap. And I choose to be free."

What temptations do you see in the paragraph above? Are any of them part of your experience? What kinds of power are talked about? The writer says he chooses to be free. How do you think he's going to manage that? How are you going to manage that? Do any of these thoughts help?

"The wicked man is doomed by his own sins; they are ropes that catch and hold him" (Prov. 5:22, *TLB*).

❋ ❋ ❋ ❋ ❋ ❋

"Do not let any part of your bodies become tools of wickedness, to be used for sinning; but give yourselves completely to God—every part of you—for you are back from death and you want to be tools in the hands of God, to be used for His good purposes" (Rom. 6:13, *LNT*).

❋ ❋ ❋ ❋ ❋ ❋

"Come and follow Me, for My servants must be where I am" (John 12:26, *LNT*).

"If you follow Me, you won't be stumbling through the darkness, for living light will flood your path" (John 8:12, *LNT*).

"Christ, who suffered for you, is your example. Follow in His steps" (1 Pet. 2:21, *LNT*).

"He will keep in perfect peace all those who trust in Him, whose thoughts turn often to the Lord!" (Isa. 26:3, *Living Ps. and Prov.*).

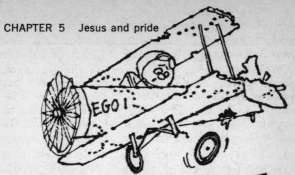

EGO TRIPS—A LONELY WAY TO FLY

Taken any ego trips lately?

That is, have you nursed your pride, fed your conceit, put somebody down in order to elevate yourself? In short, have you built up your own ego at someone else's expense?

Now, being egotistical is a definite no-no for most people and it is especially bad for Christians. The believer in Christ is supposed to be humble. He's supposed to be modest, meek, lowly, unassuming. The Christian's ego is something that is supposed to be squashed, chopped, squeezed, controlled and in some circles, obliterated.

Trouble is, for a lot of people the problem isn't an overinflated ego. It's the reverse. A lot of people —including many Christians—feel inferior, afraid, inadequate. This is exactly what makes many of these people hostile, aggressive, pushy. They're trying to cover up by coming on strong. Somehow, they hope to prop up a sagging self-image. They take ego trips because they think it might help them face that big, bad competitive world.

So where does this leave the Christian believer—especially the one who wasn't oozing with self-confidence before he believed and things haven't really gotten that much better since? For so many people the church has painted a picture that describes the Christian as one whose troubles are over and who is triumphantly facing life filled with the Spirit, dealing justly and fairly with everyone he knows and walking humbly with his God. (See Mic. 6:8.)

But it isn't that simple and most people—even church pillars—would admit it (if they didn't think any of the other pillars were listening). One of the big fallacies in Christian circles is to equate righteousness before God with righteousness before men. The Gospel guarantees righteousness before God on the basis of faith in Christ (Rom. 3:21-31).

By God's grace—His mercy and unmerited favor—we can have salvation in Christ (Eph. 2:8,9). Salvation is a free gift. God attaches no strings to His offer, but sometimes *we do*. We try to live righteously as "good Christians should." The result is that we sometimes feel guiltier *after* accepting Christ than we did *before*.

Take, for example, the true account of a Christian businessman who was commuting home from downtown New York. He was planning to hurry home for dinner and then get over to midweek prayer meeting where he was slated to lead the Bible study.

He got in the line headed for the escalator that would take him to his bus. Just as he got to the head of the line where he could board the escalator a woman with a hard face and an even harder elbow shoved in front of him. She planted that hard elbow square in his stomach as they stepped onto the escalator. So here this Christian gentleman was, riding along on the escalator with the woman's elbow firmly implanted in his tummy. Several thoughts came to his mind about what he should say to the woman. His first thought was along the lines of what he'd *really* like to say but he didn't think he could talk that way anymore.

What do you say to a hard-elbowed lady?

Then he went to the other extreme and thought about being humble, sweet and loving—sort of a modern-day version of St. Francis of Assisi. But he didn't feel humble, sweet and loving.

And so, like most of us, he had to land somewhere between the two extremes. He had to do the best he could with the situation. He removed the woman's elbow from his midsection and said with elaborate sarcasm, "Forgive me, I didn't mean to shove you."

The elbowed Christian was sure the woman would get the message. She would catch the note of sarcasm and be properly (but not too rudely) reprimanded. She should go on her way, a sadder and wiser person who would not be so quick to shove into line the next time.

Not so. The woman thought he was being sincere! Her hardened face seemed to fall apart under the shock, as she said, "I don't understand it. Why are you so nice to me? I was really rude—I shouldn't have shoved in line like that."

Now it was our Christian friend's turn to be taken aback. He had been something less than humble and loving as he had tried to cut his way through an awkward situation with some razor-sharp sarcasm. But here this woman was, reacting to his counterfeit display of love as if it had been real, and it had transformed her—at least momentarily.

Suddenly the Christian man saw her not as just a rude woman who was trying to trample him, but as someone who had been fighting all her life for a place in line. This was possibly the very first time anyone had ever stepped back and given her a place in line without a fight. And at that moment the Christian commuter felt doubly guilty. He saw how petty he had been. He felt compassion for the woman, but he also was confused and embarrassed. His profound rejoinder was: "It doesn't hurt to be nice to people." Just then they came to the top of the escalator and he ran for the safety of the bus headed for his suburb.[1]

We all want to take ego trips

Life being what it is, we all are tempted to take ego trips every day of our lives. It seems we are tempted just about every minute. The temptation to put pride ahead of God is just as universal as the temptation to live for pleasure and power instead of Him. That's why pride—a super ego trip—was the third and final basic temptation faced by Jesus as He and Satan had their little duel in the wilderness.

The count is two strikes on Satan. He tried to get Jesus to put physical pleasure ahead of God and Jesus told him that man does not live by physical pleasure alone. He tried to get Jesus to put power (doing His own thing) ahead of God. Instead, he learned that Jesus is interested in worshiping God and that nothing else in His life will become an idol no matter how much power, how much control it might give Him.

Now, in this third and final temptation, Jesus is high on the roof of the Temple in Jerusalem. And Satan says, "If You are the Son of God, jump off! For the Scriptures say that God will send His angels to guard You and to keep You from crashing to the pavement below!" (Luke 4:9-11, *LNT*).

If you like alliteration you can say the first temptation involved *pleasure,* the second had to do with *power* and this third invitation centers on *pride,* or if you like, *prestige*—roughly interpreted, an ego trip.

Just as with the other two temptations, Jesus is out of our league but not out of our ball game. Because of His great power, Satan is tempting Him in ways we would never be tempted but we can still make the application and see the connection.

Jesus and Satan are at the pinnacle of the Temple where Solomon's porch and the royal porch meet. Because the temple was built on Mount Zion in Jerusalem, it was a sheer drop of 450 feet into the Valley of Kidron, below the city.

So when Satan asks Jesus to jump, he's not suggesting a ten-foot fall that might result in a broken leg. Four hundred fifty feet is the height of a forty-five story building. This is to be a real spectacular. And Satan sweetens the pot by pointing out to Jesus that people down below will see Him jump and of course just as Scripture says, the angels will keep Him from harm and everyone will be duly impressed. In fact, the word will get around and all Jerusalem will soon be flocking to Him, and then all of Palestine, and then, who knows?

Satan usually makes such good sense

It all seems quite logical (Satan usually does make excellent "sense"). Hasn't Jesus come to bring the Kingdom of God on earth? Doesn't He want men to follow Him? He certainly has the power to leap from the 450-foot pinnacle and land unharmed. Besides, this would be an excellent way of separating Himself from false messiahs and proving that He is the real thing.

False messiahs were continually popping up in Palestine. Because the Jews kept looking for "the man sent from God" who would deliver their nation and restore it to its former glory, various characters would try to fill the role. A man named Theudus had led a group of people out to the Jordan River where he promised to split the waters of the Jordan in two with a single command. The river kept flowing as before and Theudus was a laughingstock.

Another man named Simon Magus had promised to fly through the air (shades of leaping off the pinnacle of the Temple) and had died in the attempt. Phonies like this had made promises, but they couldn't produce. Here was Jesus' chance to separate Himself from the phonies and to prove to everyone that He *could* produce anytime, anywhere, with anything.

And so Satan has the scene set for a really, really big show, and he's making it look like it will turn out to be the public relations event of the year as far as Jesus' ministry is concerned.

But Jesus isn't going to take the bait—for at least two reasons. For one thing, anyone knows that whenever you try to get a following by putting on sensational acts or coming through with super-colossal accomplishments, you're headed down a dead-end street. There is just no future in being a sensationalist. This week's scream of enthusiasm for your sensational act will be next month's yawn of boredom as your followers ask you, "What are you going to do for an encore?"

But even more important, you don't use God's power to impress people with sensational feats. Check the Gospel for yourself: Whenever Jesus performed a miracle, He did it to *help* people, not impress them.

And so Jesus answers Satan with the perfect put-down: "Don't experiment with God's patience" (Luke 4:12, *LNT*). The literal translation of the Greek says, "Do not make trial of the Lord your God." The point is that no man is to ever "put God to the test."

As with the other two temptations Jesus answers Satan from the words of Scripture. Here He is quoting Moses from Deuteronomy 6:16. In the sixth chapter of Deuteronomy Moses outlines the purpose of the Law for the Israelites. He tells them that Jehovah is their God—their *only* God. They must love Him with all their heart, soul, and might. And they must teach their children to do so as well.

Then Moses goes on to mention that the Israelites should serve only the Lord their God and not go after other gods of the people round about them (vv. 13,14). He mentions that the Lord God is a jealous God and then he says in verse 16 that the Israelites should not put their Lord and God to the test as they tested Him at Massah.

What had happened at Massah? Moses is referring to an incident that had occurred over thirty years before when the Israelites were wandering in the wilderness before being allowed to enter the Promised Land. They camped at a spot called Rephidim and there was no water. The people got thirsty, then frustrated, then angry. They grumbled and then threatened to stone Moses unless he gave them water. Moses prayed to God and asked for help. God told him to go stand upon a rock at Mount Horeb nearby and strike the rock with his rod. Moses did as God commanded and water poured from the rock.

Moses named the place *Massah*, which means "tempting Jehovah to slay us." He also referred to it as *Meribah*, which means "argument" or "strife" because it was at Massah that the people of Israel had argued against God and tempted Him to slay them by saying, "Is Jehovah going to take care of us or not?" (See Exod. 17:7, *TLB*).

And so Jesus answers Satan's slightly sarcastic but clever use of Psalm 91 with these words from the pen of Moses. And it's a perfect put-down. Satan had been there through all of the trial and trouble of the wanderings in the wilderness by the Israelites after they had come out of Egypt. He had been there tempting them, helping them feel abused, irritated and mistreated. He had been there at Rephidim helping them get angry enough at Moses to want to stone him because they were dying of thirst. Satan knew exactly what Jesus meant—and he had no comeback.

Satan suggested that Jesus take a little ego trip and Jesus replied by saying in so many words that ego trips are not for people who love God and seek to serve Him. Ego trips are another way of playing games with God and testing His patience.

Ego trips come in all sizes, lengths, shapes. The temptation to take an ego trip is ever with us and we all take a few daily. Perhaps one reason we like to ride the ego trip train is that we really don't believe we are very much after all, and if we can possibly patch up our well-punctured balloon of pride, we can have enough going for us to face the world for one more day.

God made you with an ego, but . . .

And of course, the One who gave us an ego, the One who is the perfect fulfillment of our ego, gets left out. There's nothing wrong with having an ego any more than there's anything wrong with having a nose, two eyes, two ears or ten fingers. That's the way God made us. But because of that sticky little problem called sin, we've drifted far from God and we tend to misuse the equipment He has given us. That's why the temptation to nurse our pride, build our prestige, to take an ego trip, is ever with us.

When Adam and Eve snacked on that forbidden fruit in the Garden of Eden (Genesis 3) they gave all of us an awful inferiority complex, and we've all been doing the best we can to conquer it. Unfortunately, we try to do it on our own and that, of course, is the biggest ego trip of all (as Peggy found out, see p. 65).

But Satan couldn't get Jesus to take an ego trip. Jesus told Satan in so many words, "Don't ask me to play your silly games with God—I've come to help men find Him, not to get My name in lights."

And so, Satan struck out. The Scriptures report, "When the Devil had ended all the temptations, he left Jesus for a while and went away" (Luke 4:13, *LNT*). One commentator interprets this verse: "So when He had gone through the whole gamut of temptation, the devil left Him for a time.'"

According to Scripture, Jesus met all the basic temptations and triumphed. But where does that leave us and how do Jesus' victories help us avoid defeat? And what about all those defeats that we've suffered and are still facing?

For one thing, to resist temptation, you need God and His Word. As powerful as Jesus was, He did not answer Satan by relying on the invincible *I*. Jesus' answers always came from the authority of Scripture—from His Heavenly Father. The space-age Christian may not be able to alter natural law or rise from the dead, but He is certainly able to rely on God's Word and God Himself.

Peggy:"... doing drugs, I was super-paranoid ..."

"When I accepted Jesus into my life, it was just like coming from dark into light. It was that much of a drastic change. When I was taking drugs, I preached love—and hated anybody who was 'straight'! All these people talk about love and peace and all that, and that's beautiful, but how many so-called hippies can say to the 'straight' guy next to them, 'I love you'? Now that I've got Jesus, I can do that, and I mean true, honest-to-goodness love, which is something I never knew before. I mean, I used to have sex like it was going out of style, but that wasn't love—that was just sex, sex with no point. Really, I've found that the only Person that meets my needs is Jesus.

"When I was doing drugs, and even in spiritualism, I was really a super-paranoid; I thought everybody was out to get me; I'd see somebody talking, and immediately imagine all sorts of things. And Christ has really reduced that. I still get pangs of it now and then, but now I can walk up to people I don't know and say 'Hi' to them, and eventually tell them about Jesus.

"My family relations have really improved: like one time recently there was an argument with my brother, and instead of my mother going off crying and me running upstairs to get my pills—we actually went out in the back yard and prayed together. I can see the world now; I'm awake, it's incredible.

"I'd like to help kids who are on drugs. I know that right now there are a couple hundred, at least, who are saying, 'I'm sick of this, I've got to get out.' They're in the same dark gloom I was in. What they're waiting for —the high that they want—is Jesus."

—Peggy Stringer, Schenectady, N.Y.²

It is one of the comic-tragedies of the day that Christians run around wringing their hands lamenting how they are tempted in this area and that. They wonder why they don't have more power to resist temptations. They wonder why the world keeps pressing them into its mold. And while they wonder they neglect God's Word or they fail to really believe that God's Word is that important.

At this point you may be thinking, "This sounds like the same pat pablum. Just read the Bible and everything will be dandy."

Not quite. Jesus answered all three of Satan's temptations with the quotations from God's Word —true. The obvious application is that we should know God's Word and it will help us resist temptation, also. But this does not mean the mere mechanical memorizing of Bible passages or reading "three chapters a day." What is really involved is *your life-style*. What is your frame of reference? What is your value system and where are you getting it?

Does your life-style leave you schizo?

Many Christians are spiritual schizophrenics. They say they are supernaturalists but they live like naturalists and humanists. You see, if you say you are a Christian—in the Biblical sense of the word—you are saying that you are a supernaturalist. That is, you believe in God—some Being beyond nature—and you believe in Christ's death and Resurrection from death, an event that is beyond natural law and rational explanations.

So on one hand, you may be claiming that you are a supernaturalist, but on the other you are quite possibly living like a naturalist or a humanist. In other words, when it comes right down to what you really do, think, and say, you place more stock in natural law (science) and the opinions of people. Your life-style puts the worship of human ideas and values ahead of the worship of God.

You don't think this is happening? Why, then, can certain superstars in the entertainment world start a whole new fashion trend with a word? Why is it that so many Christians can rattle off vital statistics on their favorite car, athlete or team but they are hard pressed to tell you where to go in the Bible to find such basic passages as the Sermon on the Mount, the Ten Commandments or Jesus' encounter with Satan and His temptation in the wilderness?

Ask yourself the question right now: "Where *do* I get my life-style? What *really* influences the way I think, talk and act?"

Temptation is a matter of choice. Everybody knows that. But the choices you make as you face temptations in daily life depend on the big choice: God's life-style or . . . ?

How will you handle it?

How would you describe your life-style? The following quotes from Scripture describe various choices in life-styles:

"For a man is a slave to whatever controls him. And when a person has escaped from the wicked ways of the world by learning about our Lord and Savior Jesus Christ, and then gets tangled up with sin and becomes its slave again, he is worse off than he was before" (2 Pet. 2:19,20, *LNT*).

* * * * * *

At one point, Jesus had been telling his disciples about how He must be killed and raised again the third day and Peter tried to talk Him out of it: " 'Heaven forbid, sir,' he said. 'This is not going to happen to You!' Jesus turned on Peter and said, 'Get away from Me, you Satan! You are a dangerous trap to Me. You are thinking merely from a human point of view, and not from God's' " (Matt. 16:22, 23, *LNT*).

* * * * * *

On the night before He was to die, Jesus and His disciples went to the Mount of Olives and into the Garden of Gethsemane: "There He told them, 'Pray God that you will not be overcome by temptation.' He walked away, perhaps a stone's throw, and knelt down and prayed this prayer: 'Father, if You are willing, please take away this cup of horror from Me. But I want Your will, not Mine' " (Luke 22:40-42, *LNT*).

* * * * * *

"That the way you live will always please the Lord and honor Him, that you will always be doing good, kind things for others, all the time learning to know God better and better. We are praying, too, that you will be filled with His mighty, glorious strength so that you can keep going no matter what happens—always full of the joy of the Lord" (Col. 1:10, 11, *LNT*).

* * * * * *

Temptation is as common as breathing. There is no easy out. Jesus urged his disciples to pray continually for strength to resist temptation. Is this part of your life-style? Perhaps you would want to use this paraphrase of part of the Lord's Prayer:

"Let nothing become a temptation that draws me away from You. Stay with me, Lord. When temptation comes, give me the strength to never give in."

CHAPTER 6

Mary, Martha and Lazarus

Nobody likes to talk about death. It's the thing we fear most. But we all have to face it—single-handedly. As some philosopher said: "Dying my death is the one thing nobody else can do for me."[1]

What is harder for many of us, perhaps, is to lose friends and loved ones in death. Being the one left behind—to mourn, to think, to be lonely, to miss the one who has died—is a bitter experience. One teen-ager put it like this:

"Bob was the only guy who ever mattered to me and now he is dead. We had gone together for four years. He went on a trip, and while driving on a lonely road in the middle of the night, he must have gone to sleep at the wheel. Next morning they found him still buckled in his seatbelt in the smashed-up car. That was all.

"Bob was going to be a missionary. Just 24 years old. He had started his training, and just a few days before it happened, he wrote that he had spent a great day with the Lord. I know he is in heaven now and is very happy there. But what about me down here? Doesn't God or anybody care about my feelings?

"When they closed the lid of that coffin and wheeled it out, I just couldn't take it thinking about that body I loved—his handsome face, his broad young shoulders—going into the ground to decay. Oh, I know Christians are supposed to think only of the resurrection part and being with the Lord. But I couldn't help it. I didn't have a smile on my lips and a Scripture verse coming out of my mouth like you hear about some Christians. Being out there at that cold cemetery was a horrible experience.

"People talk about faith, and I was always so sure I had a lot of it—until this happened. Now I'm not so sure. I can't figure out why God let it happen. I'm so tired—tired of hearing people say, 'Lynn, it must be the will of God.' I'm tired of people running around quoting the verses I already know by heart, especially Romans 8:28. I *know* there is a purpose in it. There *has* to be."[2]

Does Lynn sound bitter? Is she selfish for asking the question, "But what about me down here? Doesn't God or anybody care about my feelings?"

Judge Lynn as you will but appreciate her honesty. She knows the Scripture verses, but she is disillusioned and in despair. How God could let this happen is beyond her comprehension.

God's ways are not her ways. She has reached the limit of her understanding. Grief has moved in and temporarily at least she asks God the question that He has never answered for anyone in this life: "Why?"

The story of Lynn and her loss of the young man she wanted to marry has many similarities to a well-known account in the New Testament—the death of Lazarus in John 11. All of the elements are there—the grief, the questions, the assurance from Scripture. Disillusionment and despair are intertwined with hope and faith.

Jesus is near Jericho when he receives word that Lazarus is seriously ill in his home at Bethany some 25 miles away. Oddly enough, Jesus waits for two days before trying to go to Lazarus. He gives a clue concerning why He waited in John 11:4. Lazarus' illness and death will result in bringing glory to God.

Jesus and his disciples finally do arrive, and while some distance from Bethany, Martha meets them. Her first words are so typical, so human: "Sir, if you had been here, my brother wouldn't have died" (John 11:21, LNT).

Martha is saying what many of us say when we are baffled and hurt and in pain: "Where were you, God, when it happened? Why did you let it happen to me?" Jesus' quiet answer is straight to the point: "Your brother will come back to life again" (John 11:23, LNT).

Martha is puzzled for a second and then she remembers her Sunday School lessons. Yes, of course Lazarus will come back. Martha is a believer in the resurrection and she knows that he will rise again at the last day. (See Dan. 12:1,2).

Jesus' reply goes beyond Martha's limited knowledge. His words put flesh and blood around the "hope of the resurrection" that she had been taught in the Jewish Scriptures. Jesus says: "I am the one who raises the dead and gives them life again. Anyone who believes in Me, even though he dies like anyone else, shall live again" (John 11:25, LNT).

Live again . . . without deep-freeze storage?

Then Jesus asks Martha a key question: "Do you believe this?" Jesus asks us the same question today. He has promised us that the bodies of those who believe in Him will live again (with no assistance from miracle drugs or deep-freeze storage). Christ is saying that death is not the end, that those who believe and trust in Him shall live on.

It's hard to say if Martha understood everything Jesus was saying, but her reply makes it clear that she *wanted* to believe in *Him*: "I believe you are the Messiah, the Son of God . . ." (John 11:27, LNT).

The rest of the story is the better-known part. After a brief encounter with Martha's sister Mary (who also lets Him know that He has come too late), Jesus goes to the tomb and asks that the stone across the doorway be moved. After a brief prayer to His Heavenly Father, Jesus shouts, "Lazarus, come out!"

Lazarus *does* come out, to the indescribable astonishment of everyone.

We are left a little speechless ourselves, but we still have questions. While the story of the raising of Lazarus is an exciting demonstration of God's power, it doesn't necessarily solve all our problems and questions about death. Today we don't see dead friends and loved ones getting up out of the coffin as the minister intones the matchless words of John 11:25: "I am the resurrection, and the life: he that believeth in me, though he were dead, yet shall he live."

So what can you learn from this incident in the lives of Mary, Martha and Lazarus? Is it simply a pat account to assure all the faithful that Christ can perform miracles? Or is there something here for us as we face the death of loved ones and friends and as we think about our own death which will come someday?

Let's go back to the story of Lynn, the young girl who lost the young fellow she loved. People kept saying his tragic accident "must be God's will."

That's a nice, solid theological statement but it's pretty cold comfort when you've lost someone you really care about.

Are tragic deaths "God's will"?

Could it possibly be that tragic deaths are *not* God's will? That's a very risky question. It isn't good Christian form to suggest that possibly some terrible tragedies and events are *not* God's will. It is much more acceptable to say that everything that happens is the will of God and that "there are many things we just can't explain."

Perhaps that unexplainable element is why we should go easy on giving God blame for tragedies. Could it be that when a young man destined for the mission field is killed in a freak auto accident that it is neither an act of God or the will of God? Could it be that it is in fact precisely the opposite? Could it be that these tragedies are against God's will and God is just as grieved about it as those who lose the loved ones involved?

But then what do you say about death? Where does God fit in? If He is in control of the universe, doesn't He share in tragic deaths? Isn't He somehow at least partially responsible?

It's easy enough to work up a nice, tight, logical argument and make God responsible in one way or another. The Bible has never tried to explain the "why" behind horror and suffering.

We do know that you can trace many tragedies back to some human fault or sin. There could very well have been human error when the young would-be missionary crashed into the tree.

Sometimes it's very hard to know just what did happen and in many cases it is impossible to know why. Behind many tragedies there is the sure element of the unexplainable.

But it does little good to explain the unexplainable by saying "it must be God's will." Christianity doesn't offer that kind of cheap explanation. What Christianity—personal faith and trust in Christ—does offer is the power to somehow face tragedies like the death of a loved one.

That's what Jesus was telling Mary and Martha. He was saying, "I am the Resurrection and the Life. If you trust Me, you'll have the strength to bear the pain and eventually the pain will turn to joy and death will turn to life because those who believe in Me will never die."

Through the Holy Spirit, the Christian is in touch with power that can transform tragic death into triumphant hope. No other religion or philosophy can offer this kind of power. The question is, are we willing to take Christ's word for it?

Sooner or later death pays us a visit and takes one of our family, a friend, a leader we respect. Perhaps death takes us. So it is not a question of how we die, when or where (as Roger can tell you —see p. 77). It is a question of how we choose to die—or how we choose to see the death of others. The answer to how we see death is usually wrapped up in how we look at life.

According to the unpopular but very plain teaching in the Scripture, each of us will spend eternity in heaven or hell. Where we spend eternity depends on what we do with Christ's offer to believe in Him and never die (John 11:25).

The Christian does not escape the sting that death brings when it snuffs out the life of a loved one or takes his own life. None of us want to die. To be human and alive and emotionally healthy is to resist the very thought of death with all of your being. But the Christian does escape another kind of sting—the much more searing pain of the hopeless despair that comes from having no promise or hope of something better and finer beyond this life.

That's what Paul was saying when he wrote, "Oh death, where then your victory? Where then your sting? For sin—the sting that causes death—will all be gone; and the law, which reveals our sins, will no longer be our judge." (1 Cor. 15:55,56, *LNT*).

Roger: "The doctors say I will die . . ."

Roger Garcia, husky, handsome high-schooler, was at a county rehabilitation ranch, sharing his faith in Jesus Christ with a group of young fellows just about his own age. There is nothing too unusual about that—except Roger had only one leg (the other had been amputated due to cancer). Roger had also been through lung surgery—cancer again. And his latest problem was inoperable cancer of the spine. What did Roger Garcia have to say about it all?

"Medically, my condition is terminal. There is nothing more the doctors can do. They say I will die.

"There is no need to be morbid. Am I really very different from you? Aren't we all terminal cases—bound to die? Who is to say anybody here will live longer than I? Face it—we are all just one heartbeat away from eternity. None of us can choose when or how we will die, but we can choose what we will die for! The important thing is to be ready . . . to live a full life for God . . . to know the Lord . . . and know where we're going when this life is over. And believe me I know!" As Roger was leaving the county ranch somebody blurted, "That guy talks like he's going to live forever!"

That's right, he will.

—Roger Garcia, San Jose, Calif.'

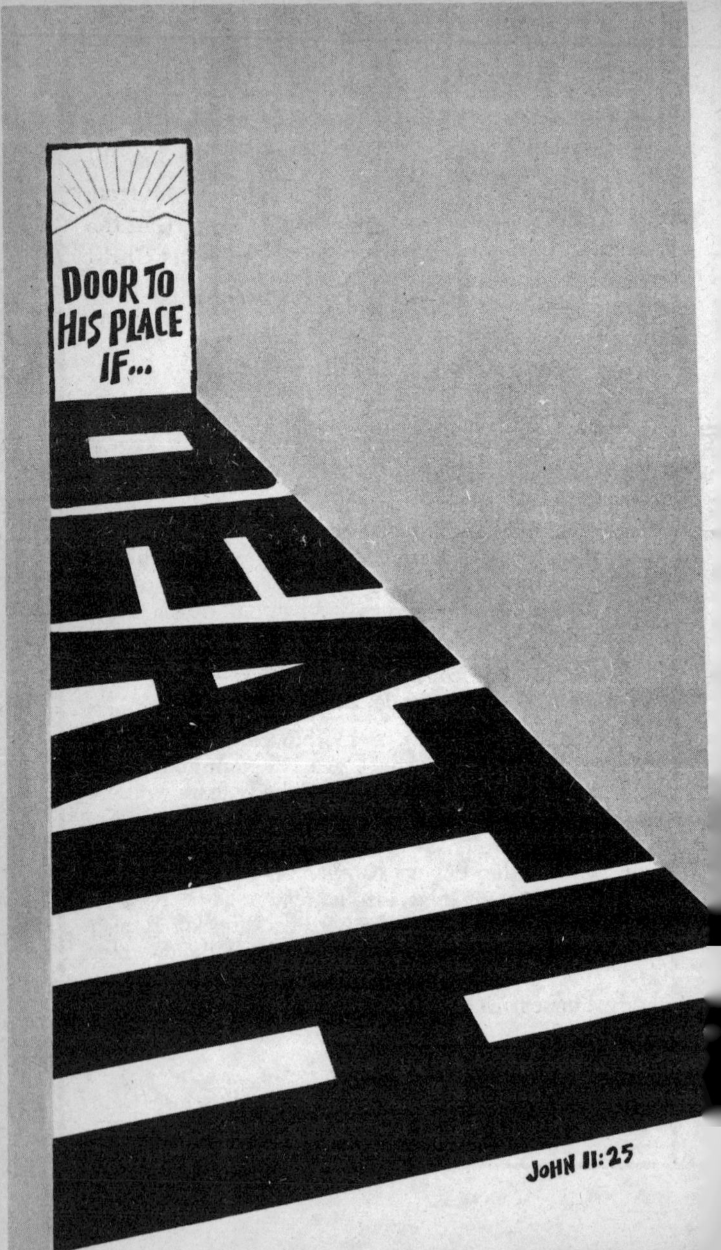
DOOR TO
HIS PLACE
IF...
JOHN 11:25

Paul knew that death was never easy, but knowing Christ does take the final sting out of it. No matter how unexplainable a death might be, the Christian can know that nothing separates him from Christ's love. "Death can't . . . separate us from the love of God demonstrated by our Lord Jesus Christ when He died for us" (Rom. 8:38,39, *LNT*). And when you know that death is no longer the last great enemy death becomes . . .

The Door to "His Place"

> Death . . . please wait.
> I have so much I want to do on Earth.
>
> But Death . . . when you do come
> Don't expect me to
> Scream
> and stamp my feet
> or
> Faint
> or run and hide.
>
> Jesus showed me what you are, Death.
> You are the door to His place . . .
> If I follow Him.
> His place that God prepared with
> Light and happiness and forever . . .
> Death . . . please wait,
>
> I'm not nearly finished here on Earth.
> But when you come . . .
>
> What do you suppose His place is like?
> — Georgiana Walker [4]

How will you handle it?

How do you really feel about death? Perhaps it is hard to put it into words. Take the following quiz and see if the thought of death has as much sting for you as it did before:

1. After reading this chapter, with the story of Lazarus and the reaction of Mary and Martha to his death, do I have less fear of dying or more fear of dying?

2. When I have to think about death, do I count on the fact that God is in charge and will bring me through even though I am afraid?

3. Do I have full assurance that when I die I will go to be with Christ—even though I don't quite know what that means?

4. What would I (or do I) think about the death of those close to me?

. . . Would I tend to feel forsaken by God for depriving me of someone I love?

. . . Would I tend to blame God for allowing a tragedy like that to happen?

. . . Would I waver between trusting God and His purposes or would I doubt that He even cares about me?

Even though I could not explain the death of someone close to me, would I still have hope that rests in Christ and be comforted by that, or would I tend to challenge God's wisdom in allowing something like that to happen?

5. Do any of the following Scripture passages give me real peace and assurance that I can trust God when death touches my life or the lives of those close to me?

"Jesus told her, 'I am the one who raises the dead and gives them life again. Anyone who believes in Me, even though he dies like anyone else, shall live again'" (John 11:25, *LNT*).

* * * ✓ * *

"When this happens, then at last this Scripture will come true—'Death is swallowed up in victory.' O death, where then your victory? Where then your sting? For sin—the sting that causes death—will all be gone; and the law, which reveals our sins, will no longer be our judge. How we thank God for all of this! It is He who makes us victorious through Jesus Christ our Lord!" (1 Cor. 15:54-58, *LNT*).

* * * * * *

"For I am convinced that nothing can ever separate us from His love. Death can't, and life can't. The angels won't, and all the powers of hell itself cannot keep God's love away. Our fears for today, our worries about tomorrow, or where we are—high above the sky, or in the deepest ocean—nothing will ever be able to separate us from the love of God demonstrated by our Lord Jesus Christ when He died for us" (Rom. 8:38,39, *LNT*).

* * * * * *

"Remember, each of us will stand personally before the Judgment Seat of God. For it is written, 'As I live,' says the Lord, 'every knee shall bow to me and every tongue confess to God.' Yes, each of us will give an account of himself to God" (Rom. 14:10-12, *LNT*).

* * * * * *

6. Finish the following in your own words: "The Lord is my Shepherd . . . even when walking through the dark valley of death I will:

_____

_____

_____

_____

81

Yes JESUS IS LORD & GOD

YOU'RE aBSOLuTeLY SuRE

NO DOUBT?

Suppose someone comes up to you and says, "I've lost my faith"? Could you help that person try to find his faith again?

Suppose this person isn't necessarily rebelling against God. Suppose it's not a case of "negative doubt" that has turned into unbelief. (For a discussion of negative vs. positive doubt, see chapter 2.)

Suppose he or she is simply being honest and open and admitting that God just doesn't seem to be there. It would be nice if He were, but it all seems so futile and useless. How can this person find a way back?

For example, a girl named Debby wrote this letter to a teen-age magazine:

"I want to believe in God, even if it seems He'll interfere. I'm a good kid . . . president of my youth group, regular churchgoer, cheerleader, straight-A student, senior class representative to student council, the whole works. I believe that the Bible is true—so what. It's never affected me anymore than a fairly interesting history book.

"Virgin birth, water to wine, rising from the dead—I believe it happened. I believe that a God had something to do with it. That is just the problem—who is 'a god'? What can a 'god' do for me or to me, or isn't he supposed to do anything but exist? How is God's love going to change me? You can't tell my 'believing' friends from my 'unbelieving' friends. I'm not afraid of dying—I'm only eighteen and science can fix me up if anything happens, so what's the use?

"That's how I feel, but everyone talks about how great and wonderful everyone is and what animals we'd be without him. I can't see what I'm missing, but there must be something that makes these people say the things they do—or are they all putting up one big front like I am?

"God has got to be somewhere, I've got to find him—I want to believe—I don't know why—I just do. I've tried to pray, but it doesn't do any good because I'm not sure of who I'm praying to or who I'm praying for—something is missing . . ."[1]

Just what do you say to Debby and people like her? (Perhaps you are asking the same questions Debby is asking.) How does the person who is searching and seeking and looking for a way to God find it? How can the honest doubter—who doesn't get satisfaction from devotional books, three-point sermons and twice-to-church-on-Sunday schedules—discover a faith that fits his or her personal needs?

There is no easy answer. It doesn't help to pat these people on the head and say, "Just believe" or "You gotta have faith." That's what they're looking for in the first place.

But it does help to remember that honest doubt is nothing new. Honest doubt was the problem of people who walked side by side with Jesus Christ during his earthly ministry. In fact, one of these men became the byword for doubt. Everybody has heard of "doubting Thomas," even the publishers of Webster's dictionary.

A lot of people remember that Thomas doubted, but a lot of them seem to forget that eventually he believed and called Christ his Lord and his God. Thomas is a profile of faith if ever there was one, and yet that profile was painted with brushes dipped in plenty of doubt.

You can pick up Thomas' story in John 14. It's the night before Jesus is to die. Thomas is with the rest of the disciples at the Last Supper. Jesus has been trying to give them final words to help them understand what is to happen and what they are to do.

Jesus has just told His disciples that they shouldn't be worried. They should trust Him. He is going to where His father lives and someday He'll return and take them too. They know where He is going and how to get there . . . (see John 14:1-4).

Thomas interrupts, "No, we don't. We haven't any idea where You are going so how can we know the way?"

Jesus' answer to Thomas is one of the best-known passages in Scripture: "I am the Way—yes, and the Truth and the Life. No one can get to the Father except by means of Me" (John 14:6, LNT).

Did Thomas understand? Scripture doesn't say, but his actions tell us that he still had questions— and doubts. Christ died on the cross the next day. Three days later Thomas heard from his fellow-disciples that Jesus had risen from the dead, that he had missed Jesus' appearance in the midst of the disciples in the upper room. Thomas wasn't sure. He just couldn't take the word of his friends that Jesus was alive.

Thomas wanted evidence—firsthand

"I won't believe it unless I see the nail wounds in His hands—and put my fingers into them—and place my hand into his side" (John 20:25, *LNT*).

A week went by. The disciples probably talked with Thomas many times, telling him again and again about seeing Jesus alive. All to no avail. Thomas would settle only for firsthand information.

Then the disciples held another meeting—behind locked doors because they were still afraid that the Jews who killed their Master would try to kill them too.

Suddenly Jesus was there! Jesus and Thomas stood face-to-face. Jesus knew what Thomas had on his mind. He invited the doubting disciple, "Put your finger into My hands. Put your hand into My side. Don't be faithless any longer. Believe!" (John 20:27, *LNT*).

Thomas was seeing for himself. At that moment Thomas was transformed from doubter to believer. *Now* he knew the way. *Now* he knew that his Lord was alive and all he could say was, "My Lord and my God!" (John 20:28, *LNT*).

If the story ended there, we could say it was an interesting story, even a fascinating one. But we couldn't find a great deal of help for ourselves. It has been almost two thousand years since any of

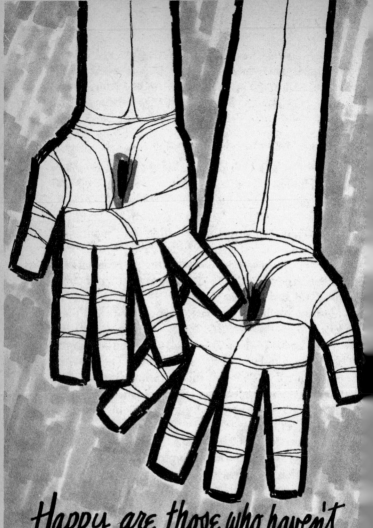

Happy are those who haven't seen... and believe anyway

John 20:29

Jesus' followers have walked and talked with him. Today we have no opportunity to "put our fingers in the nail-holes." That's what makes Jesus' next words to Thomas so important: "You believe because you have seen Me. But blessed are those who haven't seen Me and believe anyway" (John 20:29, LNT).

It sounds as if Jesus is rapping Thomas' knuckles a bit. But He is also saying that the very apostles who walked with Him, talked with Him and even saw Him risen from the dead had no real advantage over Christians today. Thomas believed because he could see and even put his finger in the nail-hole if he wished. But Jesus told him that faith doesn't need to see. Faith is believing in God, even when you can't see for yourself firsthand.

As the writer to the Hebrews put it: "To have faith is to be sure of the things we hope for, to be certain of the things we cannot see" (Heb. 11:1, TEV).

That isn't double-talk. The Bible teaches that through faith you can know. Through faith you can be sure even though you can't see or touch what you are supposed to believe in.

The same writer to the Hebrews said: "No man can please God without faith. For he who comes to God must have faith that God exists and rewards those who seek Him" (Heb. 11:6, TEV).

If you believe God exists He will reward your search. He has provided the evidence—in creation, in His Word, in the changed lives of others. You can have the assurance that you have found Him—if you want it.

Remember Debby and her honest admittal of doubt? She says she believes in the Bible, the Virgin Birth, the miracles—that Christ rose from the dead. Yet, she admits that it's all one big front. God just doesn't seem to really be there. God isn't doing anything for her. She says the Bible is true, but "so what?"

Debby's dilemma of doubt accurately describes the condition of many who try to follow Christ. Agreeing to a creed is one thing. Trusting your eternal soul and destiny to a report that a man actually conquered death is something else.

Perhaps some people don't doubt enough

What does it mean to doubt enough? Doubt is wholesome if it leads to real concern and thorough investigation. If you really care you'll investigate seriously just what you are supposed to be believing in and what difference it is all supposed to make. Perhaps a lot of Christians go through the religious motions apathetically and uninvolved because they haven't really answered that big question that Thomas had to have an answer for: "Was Jesus only a man or something more? Is the Resurrection *really true?*"

While you can't go to a film library and get an instant replay of Christ's Resurrection, there is plenty of evidence you can consult. That evidence is so overwhelming and so convincing that complete skeptics have found God because of it. A general named Lew Wallace decided to discredit the claims of Christ once and for all. He did some thorough research and wound up a Christian and the author of the famed Christian novel, *Ben Hur*.

A lawyer named Frank Morison also had his doubts about Jesus Christ. Morison respected Christ and even held Him in reverence, but the agnostics of his day had done a thorough job of undermining any beliefs he might have had in Christ's Resurrection or other miraculous elements in the Bible.

Morison decided to write a report on what he thought was a supremely important and critical phase in the life of Christ—the last seven days before the crucifixion. He applied all his legal skill and techniques of analysis to the Gospel accounts of the last seven days. He tried to take this last phase of Jesus' earthly life and "strip it of all of its overgrowth of primitive beliefs and dogmatic suppositions."

But the more Morison studied the less "disproving" of the Resurrection he did. On the contrary, the evidence began to mount up. The impossible started to look logical.

He concluded his book *Who Moved the Stone?* with this: "There may be, and, certainly is, a deep and profoundly historical basis for that much disputed sentence in The Apostles Creed—'The *third day* He rose again from the dead.' "[2]

Like Thomas, Frank Morison just couldn't believe the Resurrection had really happened. His lawyer's mind demanded evidence. Morison got that evidence by examining the eyewitness accounts written by John and other disciples.

Morison came to a life-shaking conclusion. Jesus

had conquered death. Only God conquers death. Jesus is truly God, not a dry and dusty phrase in a creed that you recite each Sunday.

When people talk about having lost their faith, perhaps many of them are really saying, "I don't have absolute proof that the Christian creed is true and it bugs me." But that's exactly what faith is—not having proof but still believing God. You can't prove your case conclusively but you don't let it bug you because you are willing to trust God and what God has said and done in Jesus Christ.

As one poet put it, "Give me faith! To trust, if not to know."[3]

And so the real question is not, "Do I have faith?" The real question is, "How did I start this journey called the Christian faith? Did I simply buy a set of doctrines and propositions? Or did I come face-to-face with a hair-raising reality: Jesus Christ died for my sins and rose again from the dead. He is my Lord and my God!"

There are light-years of difference between the two.

The Christian magazine to which Debby wrote her letter sent two staff writers out to talk to her about her problem. It turned out that her real problem was that she had become too busy with cheerleading, the student council and being president of "about a million" clubs. As a younger teenager Debby had felt close to God—that He was real. She ". . . was going to be the greatest missionary this world had ever seen."

But her busyness produced a barren life—barren as far as God was concerned and the visitors from the magazine pointed out to her that she had become so involved in her activities that they were now more important to her than God.[4]

Debby's experience is a common one. It demonstrates that believing in Christ is not the end but the beginning. That first step of faith is the start of a journey that lasts the rest of your life on this earth. Few Christians travel that road without a few doubts crossing their minds. And it's very possible to take some side roads that lead you farther and farther into the land of doubt. That's what happened to Debby.

By contrast Alison, another teen-ager, also has her doubts. She conquers them by staying in touch with God through prayer and thinking about what He's done in her life. (See p. 92.)

Everybody is different, but when it comes to faith perhaps all of us are the same. The very word *faith* implies that you are talking about something you can't prove in a rational scientific way. That's why the Bible describes faith as something that makes the unreal real and the unseeable seeable.

If faith were something that left no question . . . if faith were something that you could "know for sure" . . . why does the Bible describe faith in terms of reality you can't see? (Take another look at Heb. 11:1, *LNT*.)

Compare your own Christian experience to that of Thomas, Frank Morison, Debby or Alison. When you talk about believing that Christ rose from the dead do you realize what you are saying?

When Thomas finally believed, his response to the evidence was not, "Well, I guess the report was

Alison: "What if the Bible is just a fairy tale???"

"Sometimes I think, 'what if the Bible's just a fairy tale somebody wrote for somebody else to read? And then some weirdo picked it up and decided to get everyone to follow this book because he liked it? What if God isn't really true? And if it's just people just trying to fool you and having a good laugh while you go through all this?' But God helps me overcome these doubts . . . just by making Himself real. He does things that just couldn't happen without Him, like healing sick people, like suddenly giving me an attitude inside, an emotion that is inexplicable, refreshing, filled-up, new, alive . . .

"When you're praying, and all of a sudden the answer comes straight from God, you just have to know that He is there and the very words of the Bible are true.

"We think we are such little, tiny people and God is so huge and far away. But God can be just as tiny as you are, He can come down to you . . . He's as big or little as He needs to be.

"Once God reaches you, even just a pin-point, you can't forget it."

—Alison Clark, Long Island, N.Y.

true after all. Glad to see you up and around, Lord." Thomas fell on his knees and uttered what we all have to say if faith is ever to grow into something that can ever overcome doubt: "My Lord and my God!"

What is it for you? Doctrines and creeds that are meaningless and unreal? Or, do the doctrines and creeds remind you of the undeniable reality of being able to say, "My Lord and my God!"

How will you handle it?

"And the third day He rose from the dead. . . ."—So what? Yes, so what? Why is this the hinge on which the door between faith and doubt swings? Well, consider . . .

Since Christ rose from the dead, He is unique. He has power far beyond any human earthly religious figure. And by believing in Him I am in touch with that power and I am promised that I will conquer death also (see John 11:25, *LNT*).

"When this happens, then at last this Scripture will come true—'Death is swallowed up in victory.' So my dear brothers, since future victory is sure, be strong and steady, always abounding in the Lord's work, for you know that nothing you do for the Lord is ever wasted as it would be if there were no resurrection" (1 Cor. 15:54,58, *LNT*).

* * * * * *

Since Christ rose from the dead it proves that His claims were true. He is God, not simply a good man and a great moral teacher.

"I and the Father are one" (John 10:30, *LNT*).

"He will even raise from the dead anyone He wants to, just as the Father does" (John 5:21, *LNT*).

"Jesus replied, 'Don't you even yet know who I am, Philip, even after all this time I have been with you?

Anyone who had seen Me has seen the Father! So why are you asking to see Him?' " (John 14:9, *LNT*).

* * * * * *

Since Christ rose from the dead, His promise of the Holy Spirit in my life is also true. I have power from the risen Christ. I have His Spirit in me and it can change me and give me strength to do what I could never do myself.

"But when the Father sends the Comforter to represent Me—and by the Comforter I mean the Holy Spirit—He will teach you much, as well as remind you of everything I Myself have told you" (John 14:26, *LNT*).

"So there is now no condemnation awaiting those who belong to Christ Jesus. For the power of the life-giving Spirit—and this power is mine through Christ Jesus—has freed me from the vicious circle of sin and death" (Rom. 8:1, 2, *LNT*).

* * * * * *

. . . If Christ did not rise from the dead, I'm wasting my time. The Christian faith is counterfeit, the biggest con game of all time.

"And you are very foolish to keep on trusting God to save you, and you are still under condemnation for your sins" (1 Cor. 15:17, *LNT*).

* * * * * *

. . . If Christ did not rise from the dead, I have good reason to "lose my faith." But if He is alive and I say I believe it, and He is my Lord and my God, that puts me one up on any doubts that try to creep in.

"But we know that there is only one God, the Father, who created all things and made us to be His own; and one Lord Jesus Christ, who made everything and gives us life" (1 Cor. 8:6, *LNT*).

* * * * * *

My personal response to "And the third day Christ rose from the dead" is:

_____So, what else is new?

_____Yes, I believe it but . . .

_____My Lord and my God!

Does Christ ever go Second Class?

Would you care to admit that you are racially prejudiced?

Careful now—Christians are supposed to love everyone and prejudice is definitely not acceptable behavior in the church—or is it?

Perhaps the church could be compared to Riceville, Iowa, a farm community, population a bit under 1,000. Until 1968, kids growing up in Riceville could have had no idea about racial discrimination. Riceville had no ghettos, campus riots—no black people. But the morning after Martin Luther King was shot, pupils in Mrs. Jane Elliott's third grade class in the Riceville elementary school wanted to know "Why did they kill a king last night?"

And so Mrs. Elliott and her students talked about "killing a king." The senselessness of hate between races hit Mrs. Elliott as never before. She asked her students if they would like to learn firsthand about prejudice. They said yes.

What could they use to separate the class? They finally hit upon the color of eyes, and the class divided quite equally between brown-eyed people and blue-eyed people.

"Because I'm blue-eyed, we'll let the blue-eyed people be on top the first day," Mrs. Elliott informed her group. And so she laid down the rules: Blue-eyed people are better than brown-eyed people . . . they are cleaner than brown-eyed people . . . they are smarter than brown-eyed people . . . blue-eyed people get five extra minutes of recess and brown-eyed people can't go back for seconds at lunch. . . brown-eyed people have to drink out of a paper cup—they can't use the drinking fountain . . . brown-eyed people have to wear a special strip of cloth around their necks to identify them as inferior.

Fun and games turn into misery

What began as a "fun game" soon turned into a very miserable day—for both groups, brown eyes and blue eyes. Mrs. Elliott never stepped out of her role and never let the students do so, either. In just a short while she saw them turn from nice, clean, intelligent, pleasant little children into "nasty, despicable third-graders." Fights broke out, people were crying, and there was a noticeable difference in just one day in performance by the group that was being discriminated against. The brown-eyed group did not go through its work cards as fast. The brown-eyed people moped around, were uncooperative, slow and in general, unhappy.

By the end of that first day, "We didn't like each other very much," reported Mrs. Elliott.

The next morning, she informed the class that she had lied to them the day before. Actually *brown*-eyed people were better than *blue*-eyed people. And so, the blue-eyed people had to wear the hated collars that identified them as the inferior group.

The blue-eyed children found out what it was like to watch the brown-eyed people get five extra minutes of recess. They found out what it was like not to be able to go back for seconds at lunch and to drink out of the paper cup at the drinking fountain. They found out what it was like to not be allowed to play with the brown-eyed people because the brown-eyed people were better than they were.

And again, in just one day, the group being treated as inferior did poorer schoolwork. They were slower, less cooperative, unhappy.

By the end of the second day, both groups had had all they wanted of prejudice. Mrs. Elliott finally stopped the roleplay that had become too real for comfort. She let the blue-eyed people take off their collars. (One little fellow tore his up with vengeance.)

The group gathered around their teacher and an actual time of reunion took place as brown-eyed and blue-eyed friends got back together again. Some girls actually wept with joy and relief.

Naturally, this experiment in teaching the anatomy of prejudice (which was broadest on ABC television in the spring of 1970) did not begin to approach what many people have experienced all their lives. But it did give the innocent, protected third-graders of Riceville, Iowa, just a taste of what prejudice is like. When it was over, Mrs. Jane Elliott's class understood just a little better what prejudice really means and how it can eat at you and work on you.

Perhaps we could use some Riceville experiments in the church. Christians don't like to admit it, but prejudice is a real problem in their fold. Christians sing about "riding a heaven-bound train" but sadly enough, a lot of passengers are going second-class (and they all aren't black, either). We tend to associate prejudice with segregation, civil rights, black versus white, the incredible exploitation and degradation of the red man, etc. Actually, prejudice doesn't need a color line. Prejudice comes from within—and we're all the same color inside.

The church started with segregation

Actually, the church started out as a segregated establishment. In those first exciting days which began with Pentecost (Acts 2) thousands of people turned to Christ. And the vast majority of these thousands were Jews. Without even trying, Christianity started as a segregated situation. Many Jews turned to Christ for salvation, but they did not leave behind the bias and prejudice and hatred they felt for Gentiles. The contempt of the typical Jew for a Gentile is well illustrated in the prayer of the Pharisee who would daily thank God that he was not a common man, not a woman, and not a Gentile—in that order.

98

But having Christianity become an elite club of "enlightened Jews" is not what God had in mind. God decided to act by bringing together a Jew and a Gentile. The Jew was Peter—that one and only apostle with a heart as big as a pumpkin (and on occasion, a brain the size of a pea). Peter had a record for showing tremendous spiritual insight and devotion at one moment (see Matt. 16:15,16) and putting his foot in his mouth the next (see Matt. 16:21-23.)

The Gentile was Cornelius, a Roman soldier living in Caesarea, 50 miles northwest of Jerusalem. Cornelius had denounced pagan gods and had become what the Jews called a "God-fearer." He believed in one God and Jewish religious ethics but was not accepted as a real Jew and did not practice Jewish customs such as circumcision and attending the synagogue.

One day, God communicated with Cornelius through a vision and told him to send men to Joppa (some 30 miles south down the coast). They would go to the home of one Simon, a tanner, and there they would find a man called Peter. They were supposed to bring Peter back to Caesarea to talk to Cornelius.

So the men left and on the next day about noon they were nearing the home of Simon the tanner. At about that same time Peter was on the roof of Simon's house having prayer. He had a vision too. He saw a great sheet lowered to earth with four footed animals in it of all kinds. There were some animals that were termed *unclean*—not fit to be eaten—according to Jewish laws.

A voice told Peter to kill some of the animals and eat them, but like a good Jew Peter declined saying, "Never, Lord . . . I have never in all my life eaten such creatures, for they are forbidden by our Jewish laws" (Acts 10:14, LNT).

The voice replied, "Don't contradict God! If He says something is kosher, then it is!" (See Acts 10:15, LNT.)

To emphasize his point, God repeated the vision three times and then the sheet was pulled up again to heaven. As Peter sat there trying to figure it all out, the men sent by Cornelius arrived. Peter went down, met the men and learned their mission. Cornelius—a Gentile—wanted Peter to come to his home and tell him what God wanted him to do.

Peter must have felt things were happening a bit fast. In less than an hour his natural Jewish prejudice had been shaken severely. First he'd had a vision telling him to eat nonkosher food.[1]

While he's still trying to figure that one out, some Gentiles come and tell him that their leader —another Gentile—wants to have instructions in how to become a Christian.

All this has got to be pretty hard on a man who's been taught never to eat nonkosher ("dirty Gentile") food. In Peter's day some Jews would go so far as to say they would never help a Gentile woman in time of childbirth because they didn't want to be guilty of bringing another Gentile into the world.[2]

But right here you have to read between the lines in the tenth chapter of Acts. For one thing, Peter is staying at the home of a tanner—a man who had to work with dead animals. According to

Numbers 19:11-13, handling the dead made a person "spiritually unclean." A rigid Jew would never accept hospitality from a tanner. But Peter had.

Also, a rigid Jew would never give three Gentiles the time of day. And he certainly would not accompany them back to the home of their master. But Peter did. Peter had his faults, but living close to Christ had left him a little more open-minded about things. That open-mindedness was allowing the prejudice to run out and the love God has for people was having a chance to get in.

So, back they all went to Caesarea, and the party included six Jewish friends that Peter asked to come along. When they got to Cornelius' home there was quite a crowd. Close friends and relatives had come to meet Peter, too. And they were all Gentiles! Peter must have wondered if God wasn't trying to integrate things just a little too fast! In fact Peter revealed his reservations by telling the group: "You know it is against the Jewish laws for me to come into a Gentile home like this. But God has shown me in a vision that I should never think of anyone as inferior" (Acts 10:28, LNT).

Having admitted this much, Peter asks Cornelius what is on his mind and Cornelius wastes no time. He tells him about his own vision and how the angel told him to find this man Peter and now he and his friends and relatives are all waiting for Peter to tell them what God wants them to know.

In a space of some 24 hours Peter is learning to undo the prejudice and hatred of a lifetime. He comments: "I see very clearly that the Jews are not

God's only favorites! In every nation He has those who worship Him and do good deeds and are acceptable to Him" (Acts 10:34,35, *LNT*).

And so Peter tells them the Good News about Jesus the Messiah, the one anointed by God with the Holy Spirit and with power . . . the one who had gone about doing good and healing those possessed by demons . . . the one who was murdered on a cross and brought back to life again in three days . . . the one who ate and drank with certain witnesses after He rose from the dead. (For Peter's complete speech, see Acts 10:36-43.)

Peter closes his speech by giving the invitation. Anyone believing in Christ will have his sins forgiven through His Name. And even as Peter utters the words, the Holy Spirit comes upon his listeners. Peter and the six men he brought along are amazed. Not only has God told Peter that nonkosher food was clean and good to eat . . . not only has God shown Peter that he could stay in the home of a tanner without being contaminated . . . not only has God led Peter to befriend some Gentiles and go with them to the home of their master, but now God grips their very beings and they are praising Him.

Peter still can't figure it all out and he's still a little unsure of what's happening (prejudice and lifetime teachings die hard). But he asks, "Can anyone object to my baptizing them, now that they have received the Holy Spirit just as we did?" (See Acts 10:46-48.) And so, mustering all of the boldness and initiative for which he was famous, Peter went ahead and baptized the Gentiles and even stayed with them several more days to instruct them further in the Way.

Now if the story had ended there in the home of Cornelius, prejudice may not have died in the early church at all. But the news spread and ". . . reached the apostles and other brothers in Judea. The Gentiles also were being converted!" (See Acts 11:1, *LNT*.)

Meanwhile, back in segregated Jerusalem

So Peter returns to Jerusalem to face the Jewish music. The charge: worshiping and fellowshiping with Gentiles—even *eating* with them! (And remember, none of the Christian brothers at Jerusalem had had any visions about sheets and nonkosher food.)

Peter is definitely on the spot. It's one thing to have a vision and get all spiritual and loving toward a few Gentiles over in Caesarea. It's another thing to go back to the big city where all your friends are strict Jewish legalists and say, "It's okay to eat pork . . . with Gentiles yet!!"

Of course, Peter could easily cop out. He could claim a "credibility gap." He could say it seemed diplomatic to deal kindly with those Gentiles at the time (after all, Cornelius was a Roman centurion), but that what he had done would have no bearing on total church policy.

On the other hand, if he wanted to be militant about it, he could simply walk out, call all of his friends in Jerusalem bigots and racists, and have nothing more to do with them.

Another thing to keep in mind is Peter's record. He'd made big promises in the past and then faded when things got tough (on the night of Jesus' trial for example—see Matthew 26).

Acts 11 reports what happened. Peter didn't argue or hem and haw around. He told about the vision with the sheet and the nonkosher food. He told about the Gentiles coming to Simon's home. He told about taking six Jewish brothers with him and going up to Cornelius' place. And then he told about preaching Christ to Cornelius and his family and friends and how the Holy Spirit had broken in. Peter's summary: "Since it was God who gave these Gentiles the same gift He gave us when we believed on the Lord Jesus Christ, who was I to argue?" (See Acts 11:17, *LNT*.)

Yes, how could Peter argue, and how could the Jewish believers at Jerusalem argue either? Peter hadn't taken six men with him to Cornelius' home by accident. According to Egyptian law (which the Jews knew well), seven witnesses were necessary to prove a case. He and his six friends made up that total of seven. But even more important, God had definitely worked and lives had been changed.

Peter won his case. "When the others heard this (Peter's testimony), all their objections were answered and they began praising God! 'Yes,' they said, 'God has given to the Gentiles, too, the privilege of turning to Him and receiving eternal life!' " (Acts 11:18, *LNT*.)

And so the infant church took a giant step forward. Peter's experience helped free Christians from the narrow prejudice that claimed Christ was *only* for Jews. Christianity now had a world view. At Joppa and Caesarea, Peter had written in bold letters the "Magna Charta" of Christian liberty. *All* men—not just some men with a certain racial background—could know God's love and salvation in Christ.

But while Peter opened the door marked "unprejudiced," not every Christian walked through. The prejudice of Jews against Gentiles died hard in the early church. Prejudice is still with us today. Some Christians still carry prejudice around and it's a heavy load. And often they are prejudiced against other Christians—of another race, of another denomination, of another particular emphasis or viewpoint, be it political, social or religious.

Whenever you start a discussion on prejudice, the first thing most people think of is black man against white man. And it's true that the black man's battle against prejudice is one of the key pieces of history being written in the very days in which you live. And, rightly or wrongly, many black people believe that when they have to battle prejudice a lot of it comes from within the Christian fold or at least from a system that is supposed to be Christian. And that makes the prejudice cut extra deep.

Even Big Lew couldn't score over the color wall

Lew Alcindor led the University of California at Los Angeles to three national basketball titles. In 1969, he signed a professional contract for over a million dollars with the Milwaukee Bucks in the

National Basketball Association and went on to have a brilliant rookie year. Alcindor has received acclaim, honor and praise throughout his life because of his basketball ability. He also knows what it is like to fight the prejudice of the system.

Alcindor got introduced to that prejudice in grade school and it continued on through high school. It wasn't wide-open warfare—at least for him. It was more like a color-wall. Alcindor learned about having white friends but not really being able to relate to them. White girls were definitely off limits.

Alcindor arrived at UCLA and found things to be no better. He retreated farther and farther into a self-sufficient shell and became interested in Islam, Malcolm X and Black Nationalism.

Finally, one Sunday morning in college, he woke up and realized he hadn't been to Mass since he had come to college. He decided his days in the Roman Catholic Church were over. He became an apprentice Muslim and later joined the Sunnite branch of Islam. As far as Alcindor was concerned the Bible had produced prejudiced, hate-filled people that he had put up with all his life.'

Lew Alcindor wrote in his autobiography that it seemed to him "there was nothing in the world as unlike Christ as Christians." You may challenge this wholesale dismissal of Christianity as illogical. You may claim that he possibly never had any relationship to Christ. But you must find it difficult to deny that he has experienced prejudice since childhood and, unfortunately, much of that prejudice was shown by people in the Christian fold.

There are other black athletes who know exactly how Alcindor feels. They know exactly what Alcindor has faced but they have chosen Christ, not a rejection of the Christian establishment. One such athlete is Bob Floyd, who won all-American honors in basketball at Augustana College. He says:

"An athlete wants to be a winner, so he practices for endless hours to attain perfection in his field. We all want to satisfy our own ego. We don't work primarily for the benefit of anyone else. The thought is, 'Me first.'

"This 'me first' philosophy filters into every area of life, and we will continue having problems until it is changed. I deeply sympathize with the plight of my black brothers who suffered much injustice at many universities. However, I don't believe that presenting a list of grievances and getting new rules passed is going to greatly affect the situation. It takes something much more basic and much more effective than that. We need people who will put Christ first and ego second."

Shades of Jesus and Satan on the roof of the Temple! (See chapter 5.) Could it be that prejudice is nothing more than an ego trip? It seems that if we can't label one another as this or that . . . if we can't put each other down and thereby elevate ourselves, we can't deal with one another. At least that's the way it seems to be among so many different groups, and ironically, that includes Christian groups as well.

The reason that it's ironic is that Christians claim to be in intimate contact with the One Who is the supreme example of putting aside the "me first" philosophy. Jesus Christ never said, "Me first." He never bought a ticket for that kind of ego trip.

If a Christian wants to, he can learn from Christ —learn to be secure. He can learn to do less getting and more giving (as Scotty did, see p. 109). He can learn to do more of propping people up instead of putting them down. He can know that he doesn't have to play those cutting little games of "one-upmanship" that are so much a part of life today in the locker room, the hallway, at the office water cooler or wherever the peer group gets together.

Prejudice is no simple problem and there is no simple solution. Prejudice is like smog—or oily sewage on the beach. Prejudice is spiritual pollution. Before white people can start being nice to black, red or brown people (and vice versa), they have to start being nice to one another.

Racial prejudice is only a symptom—a sore oozing pus—that reveals what is wrong deep within. As Jesus said, "It is the thought-life that pollutes. For from within, out of men's hearts, come evil thoughts of lust, theft, murder, adultery, wanting what belongs to others, wickedness, deceit, lewdness, envy, slander, pride, and all other folly" (Mark 7:20-22, *LNT*).

"All other folly" certainly must include prejudice. You don't have to be against open housing to be prejudiced. What about your own particular clique? There's that unspoken agreement that says: "Nobody gets in unless they walk, talk, dress, think, etc., etc., just like we do—in a way that pleases us and makes us feel good."

Scotty: "With Christ, we're doing our thing."

Scotty Parsons knows what it means to be part of the world's problems. Until 1967, he was an influential gang member on Chicago's South Side (even though, at 6'4", he was simultaneously winning all-conference, all-city and all-state recognition in both basketball and football at Morgan Park High School).

Then Scotty Parsons found Jesus Christ. He says, "When you become a Christian, you have a great new awareness and outlook on the world. For the first time you can answer the question, 'What is my purpose for being here?'

"Well, I loved my friends in the gang, and I still do. Should I just let them go downhill and eventually die without God? No, I've got to seek them out and tell them what Christ is all about.

"Some kids say Jesus Christ is dead. No, man, God is alive, and we're part of a whole family doing our thing. We're telling others about him.

"Jesus Christ was a revolutionary; he advocated change. And like him, we are faced with problems of war, of poverty, of racism and separation . . . we don't just let these things go. We Christians must be part of the answer, and lead the people. Now is the time for true Christians to rise up and tell what Christ says about these problems. In fact, we've got to compensate for past years when nothing was done about hatred and discrimination, even though Jesus condemned such evils. We've got to make up for lost time.

"We don't just sit and do nothing in a world that needs help as bad as this one. With Christ, we're doing our thing."

—Scotty Parsons, Chicago, Illinois[4]

Prejudice is Spiritual Pollution

ACTS 11:17

So how do you clobber your clique and its prejudiced pastimes?[5] Do you tell all your friends (those in your clique) to get lost? Does that really accomplish much?

Choose between hate-prejudice and love-prejudice

There is another possibility. The philosopher Benedict Spinoza had a theory that allowed for two kinds of prejudice. There is *hate-prejudice* which thinks ill of others without sufficient warrant. There is also *love-prejudice* which *thinks well of others without sufficient warrant.*

Could it be that Christians have the power to practice love-prejudice? After all if a person names the name of Christ and claims that God loved him enough to die for him shouldn't he be able to look at others and feel love-prejudice toward them rather than hatred? In other words, shouldn't he be able to love these people without sufficient warrant or reason?

It's practically impossible to go through life "unprejudiced." Why not turn some of that hate-prejudice to love-prejudice? After all, love-prejudice is the kind God showed toward us. God so loved the world without sufficient reason that he sent his only Son to die for all of us (John 3:16). Jesus taught us the same thing when he said, "Treat others as you want them to treat you" (Luke 6:31, LNT).

The choice is there: you can practice hate-prejudice or you can try God's way with love-prejudice.

Is it worth it to argue?

How will you handle it?

What can you do about prejudice?

Read the following "contract," and see if you want to sign it (or any part of it).

I could go to the library (or elsewhere) this week to find books and magazines to bring me up to date and keep me informed on the racial situation and minority group problems.

I could try to begin establishing a meaningful relationship with a person I believe is being treated as a second-class citizen. And I could make the first move. I could listen and try to understand the viewpoint of a person who differs from me in race, belief, dress or background (someone I might be prejudiced against).

I will speak out this week when I hear statements from people expressing prejudice toward others.

I will pray every day and ask the Holy Spirit to work in my life to make me sympathetic and loving toward people of other races and beliefs (love-prejudice).

I will spend some time every day thinking about my own attitudes and thoughts to see if there are any contradictions between what I know about God's love and what I feel toward others.

I will ask God to reveal specific prejudices in me that I should try to get rid of.

I will make an agreement with God to work especially on these three ideas this week:

_____

_____

_____

Signed:_____

For more ideas on what the Bible teaches about prejudice see Luke 10:25-37; John 4:1-24; James 2:1-9.

WITNESSING:

WHAT YOU SAY OR WHAT YOU DO?

What's more important when you witness for Christ? What you *say* . . . or what you *do*?

In other words, is it more important to have a good line . . . or live a good life?

Most Christians would like to be more effective witnesses, but witnessing seems to be like the weather. The church (especially the pastor) talks a lot about it, but many Christians aren't sure they are doing much about it. Many Christians aren't even sure they know what witnessing *is*.

One thing a lot of believers feel quite sure about, though, is that the "Brother, are you saved?" technique is not for them. It may have worked fifty or a hundred years ago, but today it just turns people off. So, rather than risk turning people off, many Christians hope to turn them on by witnessing with their lives, their actions. "It's far more important," runs the argument, "to live like a Christian than to talk about it all the time."

113

Will the silent majority please speak up?

The result is a vast Christian silent majority. Not only do many Christians fail to talk about their faith; they wouldn't know what to say if someone asked them to.

Yet the Lord Himself left us our orders . . . to be witnesses for Him . . . everywhere we can (see Acts 1:8). If you bother to look up the word *witness* in Webster's dictionary you learn what it means "to testify, to give evidence, to attest, to share personal knowledge of something."

So it seems that while *actions* are certainly important, witnessing just naturally includes having *answers,* as well.

Is there a model—a prototype—who can help us hit the elusive happy medium? Scripture describes many "model witnesses." For example, there was Peter . . . and Paul. A bit on the "come on strong" side, perhaps. Besides, they were apostles—professional preacher types, you might say. Very dynamic and all that, but not too easy to identify with.

Well, there was Stephen . . .

Stephen? Let's see, now. A deacon in the early church, wasn't he? A layman, who had the rather dull job of feeding widows and other welfare cases. You can pick up Stephen's story in Acts, chapter 6. He was part of the Christian church that formed in Jerusalem in those exciting days right after Christ's ascension and the day of Pentecost. (See Acts, chapters 1 and 2.)

As anyone who has been in any organization can tell you, bringing people together and working together presents problems. One of the problems in the early church was that there were a certain number of Christians who had no means of making a living. A lot of them were widows who could not work; some were probably sick or incapacitated in one way or another. And so the church had its own welfare program, which it copied from Jewish customs. People with permanent support problems received food and money from the church each week —enough for fourteen meals or two meals a day.

Keep in mind that almost everyone in this first Christian church in Jerusalem was a converted Jew. There were two kinds of Jewish converts in the church. There were *Jerusalem Jews,* who took great pride in being true Hebrews because they or their families had always lived in Jerusalem (for many generations).

There was also a group called *Hellenist Jews,* Greek-speaking people who had come to Jerusalem from various foreign countries and had stayed on after becoming Christians. It seems there was a bit of friction between Jerusalem Jews and Hellenist Jews. Soon the Hellenists were complaining that their widows were not being treated fairly in the church's welfare program. (See Acts 6:1.)

Let's work together

And so the apostles called a meeting and decided to appoint seven deacons to take care of practical matters such as feeding the widows and other needy people. Among these seven was "Stephen (a man unusually full of faith and the Holy Spirit) . . ." (Acts 6:5, *LNT*).

Stephen and the others did their job well but Stephen wasn't content with simply helping to run breadlines and to distribute food. Acts 6:8 reports that Stephen was so full of faith and the Holy Spirit's power that he did spectacular miracles among the people. He also started witnessing in various parts of the city.

One day Stephen got into an argument with a group of particularly militant Jews, non-Christians who were called the "Freedmen." (See Acts 6:9.) When the Freedmen couldn't win any points in their arguments with Stephen they decided to cook up some false charges against him, claiming that he had cursed Moses and even God. They got him arrested and brought before the Jewish Sanhedrin where he stood trial.

So, Stephen had his day in court. He had the opportunity to be a witness indeed. The charge: Stephen had constantly spoken against the Temple and against the laws of Moses. Stephen had supposedly said that some fellow named Jesus of Nazareth would destroy the Temple and throw out all of Moses' laws. (See Acts 6:13,14, *LNT*.)

Stephen didn't take any Fifth Amendments. In fact, almost all of the seventh chapter of Acts is devoted to his testimony. Stephen tailored his Christian witness to his audience—an audience of Jews who were steeped in Bible history.

"The glorious God appeared to our ancestor Abraham . . ." he began, and he went right on through centuries of Jewish history, reminding his listeners that God had worked personally with people throughout all time. Stephen reminded the court of Isaac, Jacob, Joseph and Moses. He reminded them that ". . . our fathers rejected Moses and wanted to return to Egypt" (Acts 7:39).

But Stephen wasn't through. He went on to talk of Joshua, David and Saul—and the Temple that Solomon had built. And then Stephen made a telling point: "However, God doesn't live in temples made by human hands. 'The heaven is My throne,' says the Lord through His prophets, 'and earth is My footstool. What kind of home could you build?' asks the Lord! 'Would I stay in it?'" (Acts 7:48,49, *LNT*).

And then Stephen laid it right on the line: "You stiff-necked heathen! Must you forever resist the Holy Spirit? But your fathers did, and so do you! Name one prophet your ancestors didn't persecute! They even killed the ones who predicted the coming of the Righteous One—the Messiah whom you betrayed and murdered" (Acts 7:51,52, *LNT*).

Witnessing results in interest, apathy or rage

There are normally three typical reactions to a Christian witness: Interest and response, apathy and turned-off indifference, or outright rage and indignation. Stephen's audience went into a rage. He had put the finger of truth on a very tender nerve. They mobbed him, dragged him out of the city and stoned him to death. And even as the stones struck him down Stephen witnessed as he prayed, "'. . . Lord Jesus, receive my spirit.' And he fell to his knees, shouting, 'Lord, don't charge them with this sin!' and with that, he died" (Acts 7:59,60, *LNT*).

And so Stephen became the first Christian martyr. And now you might be thinking, "Good grief! Do I have to be martyred in order to be a good witness?" Perhaps. There are Christians who are being martyred today because of their faith. What God's will is for you is hard to say. Few people in the Western part of the world get martyred because they witness for Christ. There are some who get persecuted, laughed at and made fun of. (Maybe *that's* what keeps a lot of us from witnessing.) But Stephen was a model witness, not because he sacrificed his life, but *because of what he said and how he lived.* Stephen put three principles into action and they are principles you can use today:

He knew the facts of his faith.

He used terms people could understand.

He pointed his listeners to Jesus Christ.

What facts did Stephen know? Are they the same facts we need to know today? Are we supposed to recite a brief history of the Jewish people every time we feel there is an opportunity to witness?

Stephen was in unusual circumstances. He had the platform and the audience for his long speech in Acts, chapter 7. In the space age sometimes you only have a few seconds to talk about Christ. Perhaps you only have until the next corner when somebody gets out of the car. Perhaps you only have a few minutes before the bell rings.

Perhaps even more to the point, you have people whose interest span is very short. Unless you can

YES, ALL HAVE SINNED.
ALL FALL SHORT OF GOD'S
GLORIOUS IDEAL. ROM. 3:23
FOR THE WAGES OF SIN
IS DEATH BUT THE FREE
GIFT ... ETERNAL
LIFE ... JESUS
CHRIST ... ROM.
6:23 ... LOVED
THE WORLD SO MUCH
THAT HE ... ONLY
SON ... NO ONE
WHO ... HIM
WILL ... BUT
HAV ... LIFE
JOHN 3:16 THERE IS
SALVATION IN NO ONE
ELSE! UNDER ALL
HEAVEN THERE IS NO
OTHER NAME FOR MEN
TO CALL UPON TO SAVE

KNOW THE FAITH

ACTS 7:55

tell your story simply and clearly and briefly, they get bored with religion. They just don't want to know that much.

But Stephen's speech is still a useful illustration. He covered thousands of years in a space of a relatively few words and that, in a way, is exactly what you have to do. But your job is even more difficult than that. You often have to deal with many people who have gotten warped ideas about Christianity. They think it is some kind of no-no religion. Many are confused on just who Jesus Christ really was. Many are turned off by "church hypocrites."

So what do you really need to know? *What facts should you be able to communicate quickly and clearly?* Dozens' of different kinds of tracts and pamphlets have been written on presenting Christ in a "plan of salvation." If you are serious at all about sharing Christ with others you should have one of these plans firmly in mind. Here is one that covers the basic points quickly and clearly. All Scripture quotations are from the *Living New Testament,* which may help you make your witness sound a little more contemporary.

FACT 1: GOD'S GOAL—ABUNDANT LIFE

God really loves you and wants to give you the abundant life—a life full and satisfying!

God's Word, the Bible, says . . .

"For God loved the world so much that He gave His only Son so that anyone who believes in Him shall not perish but have eternal life" (John 3:16).

"My purpose is to give eternal life—abundantly" (John 10:10).

What keeps people from experiencing the abundant life?

FACT 2: MAN'S HANG-UP—SEPARATION BY SIN

God made man with a free will. Man chose to reject God's love and disobey God. This disobedience, called sin, separates man from God. Today man still chooses to disobey.

The Bible says . . .

"Yes, all have sinned; all fall short of God's glorious ideal" (Rom. 3:23).

"The wages of sin is death, but the free gift of God is eternal life through Jesus Christ our Lord" (Rom. 6:23).

Man has failed to solve the sin hang-up, but God has the solution.

FACT 3: GOD'S SOLUTION—JESUS CHRIST

The only solution to the sin hang-up is Jesus Christ.

When Jesus Christ died on the cross in our place, He paid the penalty for our sins. He bridged the gap between God and man.

"God is on one side and all the people on the other side, and Christ Jesus, Himself man, is between them to bring them together" (1 Tim. 2:5).

"But God showed His great love for us by sending Christ to die for us while we were still sinners" (Rom. 5:8).

"Jesus told him, 'I am the Way—yes, and the Truth and the Life. No one can get to the Father except by means of Me'" (John 14:6).

Christ doesn't force himself upon man. Man must choose whether or not to receive God's solution.

FACT 4: MAN'S RESPONSE—RECEIVE CHRIST

You must decide that you want to turn from sin to God. You must personally invite Christ into your life and trust Him as Lord of your life.

"Now change your mind and attitude to God and turn to Him so He can cleanse away your sins and send you wonderful times of refreshment from the presence of the Lord" (Acts 3:19).

"Believe on the Lord Jesus and you will be saved . . ." (Acts 16:31).

"But to all who received Him, He gave the right to become children of God. All they needed to do was to trust Him to save them" (John 1:12).

"Four Facts God Wants You to Know"[1] is a basic presentation of how to lead someone to Christ. If a person wants to become a Christian, he should be led in a prayer that helps him admit his sin and his determination to turn from sin (repentance). He should tell God He believes Christ died for his sins and he should ask God to come into his life. Here's a sample prayer that can be used:

"Lord Jesus, I confess that I am a sinner. I need help with my hang-ups. I believe that You died for me and I receive You right now. Come into my life and take control. Help me to become the kind of person You want me to be. Thank You for loving and forgiving me."

But perhaps the "Four Facts" have a bit of a "canned" sound. You agree that all four points are important, but you need a little something more to talk about just how Christ makes a difference in life. Following is an approach that incorporates the same basic ideas and Scripture references as the "Four Facts." There is, however, a little more emphasis on the benefits in knowing God through Christ and explaining concepts and terms as you go.

To be a Christian is . . .

To be a Christian is to be a follower of Jesus Christ, a man who claimed to be God and who proved He is just that. To be a Christian, then, is to be in touch with the living God. I have a direct line, so to speak, to the One Who "made it all"—including me. That means I know the One Who created life and knows how it should really be lived. Jesus said, "My purpose is to give eternal life —abundantly" (John 10:10, *LNT*).

Being a Christian doesn't make me perfect, but it puts me in touch with the One Who is perfect, the One Who will help me become what I should be.

"For because of our faith, He has brought us into this place of highest privilege where we now stand, and we confidently and joyfully look forward to actually becoming all that God has had in mind for us to be" (Rom. 5:2, *LNT*).

The reason I feel that believing in and following Jesus Christ puts me in touch with the God who made the universe is because Christ lived on this earth and proved that He is God by rising from the dead. The Resurrection of Christ was a miracle—a supernatural event that you can't explain in scientific terms. But if we're talking about knowing the God who made the universe then we are talking about Somone far beyond nature and natural law— someone SUPERnatural.

According to the Bible, God became a man in the person of Jesus Christ.

Jesus said, "I and the Father are one" (John 10:30, *LNT*), and "Anyone who has seen Me has seen the Father!" (John 14:9, *LNT*).

Jesus lived on this earth, performed miracles, died on the cross for my sins and rose again from the dead—final proof that he has conquered death and that He is God.

"Christ died for our sins just as the Scriptures said He would, . . . He was buried, and . . . three days afterward He arose from the grave just as the prophets foretold" (1 Cor. 15:3,4, *LNT*).

Because I believe this, I trust Christ to be my connection with the God who made it all. Before I knew Christ I didn't have any connection, because sin separated me from God.

When I talk about "sin" I don't mean particular acts of wrongdoing, disagreeable social habits or immoral practices. My sin is between me and God. Sin means that I am in rebellion against Him. I can rebel against Him actively . . .

"But those who keep on sinning are against God, for every sin is done against the will of God" (1 John 3:4, *LNT*).

Or I can rebel passively . . .

"Remember, too, that knowing what is right to do and then not doing it is sin" (James 4:17, *LNT*).

God is the One Who decided what is against His will and what is not right. He made the universe. He made me. He has His own standard that He wants me to live up to. That basic moral standard is built into every human being who ever lived. We all know when we have been cheated or when we have been wronged in some way. Nobody approves of murder, stealing, lying, etc. There may be people who do these things, true, *but they don't want it done to them.* Unfortunately, no person matches God's standard.

"All have sinned; all fall short of God's glorious ideal" (Rom. 3:23, *LNT*).

It is like God is on one side of a raging river, and

I'm on the other. I'd like to get over to Him but I can't. It's too far to swim, the current's too swift and the water is deep. But Jesus Christ is like a bridge that reaches from my side to God's side.

"God is on one side and all the people on the other side, and Christ Jesus, Himself man, is between them to bring them together, by giving His life for all mankind" (1 Tim. 2:5,6, *LNT*).

Jesus Christ then is my bridge over troubled water. I believe it made a difference when He gave His life because He was God Himself. Because He was God Himself He could die for my sins—everybody's sins, as a matter of fact. And because He was God He could rise from the dead and give me the promise that I too can have eternal life.

Maybe you want to know why I want eternal life. I want it because it will be far better than this life. Even though I am connected to God now . . . even though I know He loves me now and it's a tremendous adventure and experience . . . it's going to be even better because, when I "die" and my soul leaves this body, I'm going to go to something far better and become completely what God wants me to be.

So, to be a Christian is not a state of "having arrived." Christians aren't perfect. Some Christians are phony, they cheat, they lie. And because people know about Christians who are this way or have done this or done that they tend to write off Jesus Christ and Christianity.

But God doesn't write people off because they aren't perfect. That was the whole point behind the coming of Christ. He left heaven, came to this planet, lived as a man, died on the cross, and rose again from the dead—all because "God so loved the world" that he wanted to reconcile it—bring it back—to Himself.

The Bible talks about "being saved." That means that I have a way out of my predicament. I have a way to handle my hang-ups. No person who is really honest is going to deny that he falls far short of what he should be and could be. Some people try to make excuses and rationalize. Some people play with words and say that they sin but they are not sinners.

But deep inside we all know what is right and wrong, and we know we have not lived up to what we know.

The Bible says that God gets us out of our predicament because of His mercy and His love.

"For God loved the world so much that He gave His only Son so that anyone who believes in Him shall not perish but have eternal life" (John 3:16, *LNT*).

I cannot earn my way to heaven. I can't possibly swim across that raging river to God's side. I have to have faith. . . . I have to believe that Jesus Christ is who He said He was and that He did what the Bible said He did.

And so I simply trust Christ to carry me across that river. *He's my bridge over troubled water.*

There's not a whole lot of self-satisfaction in that. I can't take any credit for it. I can't get admiring looks that tell me I'm cool and clever because of what I've done. I didn't do it. I can only accept it.

"Because of His kindness you have been saved

through trusting Christ. And even trusting is not of yourselves; it too is a gift from God. Salvation is not a reward for the good we have done, so none of us can take any credit for it" (Eph. 2:8,9, *LNT*).

But even though I am a Christian—even though I believe in Christ—I still slip sometimes. I mess myself up real good. But even though I have a short circuit now and then, I know I'm wired directly to God through Jesus Christ.

"My new life tells me to do right, but the old nature that is still inside me loves to sin. . . . Who will free me from my slavery to this deadly lower nature? Thank God! It has been done by Jesus Christ our Lord. He has set me free. For the power of the life-giving Spirit—and this power is mine through Christ Jesus—has freed me from the vicious circle of sin and death" (Rom. 7:25; 8:2, *LNT*).

So, to be a Christian is to be someone who is in direct *contact* with the God who has made it all—contact through the Person of Jesus Christ.

To be a Christian is to be someone who can turn to the very source of the universe with his questions, his problems, his weaknesses.

"But if we confess our sins to Him, He can be depended on to forgive us and to cleanse us from every wrong. [And it is perfectly proper for God to do this for us because Christ died to wash away our sins]" (1 John 1:9, *LNT*).

To be a Christian is not to be perfect, but to be in direct contact with the One Who is perfect.

To be a Christian is to be someone who is growing, changing and becoming—more loving, more concerned about others, less centered on yourself.

Sometimes I don't see tremendous change but I know that as I walk after the Holy Spirit and let Him fill my life, He will bear His fruit: love, joy, peace, patience, kindness, goodness, faithfulness, gentleness and self-control.

To be a Christian is to be someone who knows that he will spend eternity with God instead of without Him.

"For the wages of sin is death, but the free gift of God is eternal life through Jesus Christ our Lord" (Rom. 6:23, *LNT*).

*　*　*　*　*　*

That's one description of what it means to be a Christian. Your description might put heavier emphasis on Jesus being your friend, or how knowing Christ gives you spiritual power to live each day. What's important, however, is to blend Biblical truth with your own feelings about your experience. (See Lonnie's testimony, p. 129.)

Of course, everyone isn't always interested. We're living in a skeptical "religion-saturated" age. A typical comeback goes something like this:

"What if it all isn't true? What if the Bible is a bunch of fairy tales? My uncle is a nuclear physicist and my cousin is into transcendental meditation and they don't dig the Bible."

Tell them they're free to question the Bible. God created all of us with a free will. He loves all of us so much He lets us make our own choice:

Reject His Word, turn away from it, and you have everything to lose.

Accept God's Word, believe it and live it, and you have everything to gain . . . and God besides!

Lonnie: "I didn't want to be like a baby . . ."

Teen-ager Lonnie Royal had been a Christian for a while when he decided he "wanted to grow and become more mature in knowing Christ; I didn't want to be like a baby all my life." Lonnie got involved in the Youth for Christ Bible quizzing competition, one of the first blacks in Tennessee to do so. In 1968, his team won third place in the entire nation and he personally received the coveted quizmaster's trophy. In 1969, the Tennesseeans were back again, this time to take second place. This excellence came at the cost of two to three hours of study per day as Lonnie virtually memorized whole books of the New Testament.

"At first I thought it might be a drag," Lonnie remembers, "but when I got into it and started studying, it really said things that relate to everyday life. The Bible has so much to say to teen-agers of the Now Generation! Times have changed, but the Bible still applies.

"There are some problems we all face as Christians, but we have a Problem-Solver. By studying the Gospel of Mark and the Epistle to the Philippians this past year, I found answers to my problems, and this has been a strength for me. For example, Philippians 1:19,20 have helped me to become unashamed of Christ. That way He can use me better; naturally, He doesn't want people who are ashamed of Him.

"If you look for something when you study and try to get something out of it (not just reading to be reading), it really comes alive; it's full of action . . . the Bible has answers for everybody's problems; we just have to search them out."

—Lonnie Royal, Soddy, Tennessee[2]

How will you handle it?

You can read about witnessing, but until you do something about it you won't get any better at it. Here are some ideas that might be useful.

1. Get together with a Christian friend and practice "leading each other to Christ." Use the "Four Facts" material on pp. 120-121 and also try working in some thoughts from "To Be a Christian Is . . ." on pp. 122-127.

2. As an experiment, see how many Christians you know who can repeat their own version of the four facts or talk about their faith in any knowledgeable way. Use a man-on-the-street approach, perhaps, and ask *Christian* friends, acquaintances, relatives, parents what being a Christian means to them and how they would explain it to somebody else. Some people will probably give you some excellent ideas that you can use yourself. Others — your parents perhaps — may be pleased or impressed if you sit down and talk to them about what it means to be a Christian.

3. Try sharing your faith with a non-Christian friend. Don't get all up-tight and tense. Just say, "Look, we're studying witnessing at my church now and I'd like to see if I could share my main beliefs with you clearly in a way you could understand." Disarm your friend by assuring him you're not trying to convert him and that if he will give you a hearing it will be a big favor to you. If you just happen to interest him in Christianity that will be the work of the Holy Spirit, Who will use what you say to speak to your friend.

4. Try writing a letter to someone you haven't seen for a while and share your faith in Christ with him. Use ideas from the "Four Facts" and "To Be a Christian Is . . ." sections of this chapter. Add your own thoughts and ideas. Writing down what you believe has tremendous benefits and it just could be that the one who receives your letter will benefit too.

IT TaKeS BoTH WINGS To GeT OFF THe GROUND

What's more important when you witness for Christ? What you say . . . or what you do?

Wait a minute . . . that's how the last chapter started . . . and it turned into a pitch for knowing what you believe—knowing the facts of your faith.

But witnessing is like an airplane. There are two wings to witnessing: *knowing what you believe* is one of them; *living what you believe*—feeling it inside to the point where it affects your attitude and actions—is the other.

Stephen—profile of faith in the last chapter—really knew his stuff and he could present it with power and conviction. Ironically enough, when Ste-

131

phen was stoned to death by the howling mob who couldn't stand before his logic and Bible knowledge, there was a young man watching—actually holding the coats of those doing the stoning. It was Saul of Tarsus—a young Jew who was a Hebrew of the Hebrews, a Pharisee of the Pharisees and a persecutor of Christians to end all persecutors. He hated Christianity and Christians with a passion. He was sure they were some kind of blasphemous cult and that God wanted him to stamp them all out.

But God had other plans. Soon after he helped dispose of Stephen, Saul decided that he would journey up to Damascus from Jerusalem to find more Christians there and to bring them back— dead or alive. But on that road to Damascus, Saul met Christ face-to-face in a flash of blinding light. Christ spoke to him from that light. Saul believed, and it was the beginning of a completely new life.

The first new thing Saul got was a Greek name— Paul. He went on from there to become the greatest witness for Christ the world has ever seen. He poured the same zeal and energy into preaching Christ as he had used when persecuting Christians. Like Stephen, he knew the facts of faith, he knew how to talk the language of his audience and he always pointed them to Christ, his Lord and Saviour.

Even Paul didn't bat 1.000

But even Paul didn't bat 1.000. Even Paul had his bad days. Even Paul learned that witnessing is more than technique and three-point formulas.

Anyone who has done any traveling, appearing in various towns as a performer or speaker, can remember the spots where he "bombed out." For Paul, one of these spots was Athens, capital of Greece and home of the intelligentsia of the day. They didn't stone him at Athens (the way they did at Lystra). They did worse. They laughed.

And yet Paul's witness to the Athenians was a model of knowing the facts, using the language your audience could understand and pointing them to Jesus Christ. When Paul arrived in Athens (on his second missionary journey), ". . . he was deeply troubled by all the idols he saw everywhere . . ." (Acts 17:16, *LNT*).

Paul didn't waste any time. As was his custom he first preached in the local synagogue and tried to persuade fellow Jews to accept Jesus as the Messiah. And then he went to the public square—the meeting place of the philosophers and the scholars. He shared the Gospel with the Epicurean and Stoic philosophers. Their reaction was something less than wild enthusiasm but they did decide Paul was interesting enough to be scheduled to appear before the Areopagus, the council of nobles who sat in court on Mars Hill to consider the latest philosophies of the day.

As Paul stood before the learned men at the Mars Hill forum, he opened his speech by saying: "Men of Athens, I notice that you are very religious, for as I was out walking I saw your many altars, and one of them had this inscription on it—'To the Unknown God.' You have been worshiping Him without knowing who He is, and now

I wish to tell you about Him" (Acts 17:22,23, LNT).

The rest of Paul's speech is in Acts 17:24-31. It is a model witness, perfectly fitted to the minds and thoughts of the Athenians who listened. Yet, Paul didn't water down the Gospel. He reminded them that God would not put up with sin—with worshiping idols made with hands. He would judge the world and He had done so in Jesus Christ, the same One He had raised from the dead.

The result? Most of them laughed, and only a handful believed. Scripture records no church starting at Athens. In spite of Paul's convincing arguments, few had been convinced.

And so Paul left Athens and went on to Corinth where he probably expected an even rougher reception than he got on Mars Hill. Corinth, you see, was the wildest city the world knew at that time. It was the original red-light district, the home of the temple of Aphrodite, the goddess of love. Worship of Aphrodite was very popular in Corinth. A lot of the people (especially the men) seldom missed a worship service. Perhaps having sexual intercourse with temple priestesses had something to do with their devotion.

And so Paul—fresh from his defeat on Mars Hill —must have had plenty of second thoughts as he trudged into Corinth. They had laughed at him in Athens. What would they do here?

But Paul made a simple vow. He was bitterly disappointed with what had happened at Athens but he was a long way from being totally discouraged.

What was that vow? Several years later, Paul wrote a letter back to the church at Corinth and told them how he had felt and what he had vowed to do: "I decided that I would speak only of Jesus Christ and His death on the cross. And my preaching was very plain, not with a lot of oratory and human wisdom, but the Holy Spirit's power was in my words, proving to those who heard them that the message was from God" (1 Cor. 2:2,4, *LNT*).

Paul is saying that you can know your facts. You should know your witnessing techniques and know some answers to questions that people might ask. But beyond all that there is something extra. You need the right attitude—an attitude that has you relying on the Holy Spirit, even when you don't feel very brilliant or convincing. Paul may have felt quite brilliant and convincing on Mars Hill. (Scripture doesn't say, but his speech *is* a model of eloquence.) But little happened in Athens.

One wing never gets you off the ground

Paul came to Corinth in fear and trembling, determined to preach Christ in the power of the Holy Spirit. The result was a church—a body of redeemed Christian believers living in the middle of the moral cesspool of its time. Even Paul, superwitness of the Christian faith—learned that witnessing is like an airplane, and all airplanes have two wings. If you try to witness with only one, you never get off the ground.

But you may find it a bit difficult to identify with Paul. You can empathize with his disappointment at Athens. You can be inspired by his determination and unbelievable courage. But oratory on Mars Hill is not your particular scene. Perhaps you will come closer to identifying with the sixteen-year-old in the following story. This isn't an encouraging "success story," but it may ring true for you because you've been there—in the same kind of situation, experiencing the same kind of frustration. In a reverse sort of way this story has a lot to say about what witnessing really is—not so much about what you are supposed to say, but how you are supposed to feel....

Spotless

By Milo Kaufmann

I had almost forgotten about the rain, I had stood by the traffic light so long. There was just a thin drizzle now. I didn't much care if a car came by right away because I had been in the rain long enough to be drenched clear through. My duffel bag was supposed to be water repellent, so I didn't worry about the things in it—mostly dirty clothes from my overnight stay at the campground.

The click beside me told me that the light was changing. That meant cars would have to stop, and they could look me over and decide whether they wanted to pick me up. I knew I must look pretty soaked by now.

I watched the green Ford coming up to the light. There was just the driver in it. He looked pretty young. Maybe he'd give me a ride.

He was going to pick me up. When he got to the light, he motioned at me with his finger. I grabbed my duffel bag and hustled to the car.

"Where you going?" the driver asked.

"Baxter," I said.

"Hop in. I'm going to Chicago. Go right through Baxter."

I tossed my duffel bag into the back and settled down in the front seat.

"What's your name, kid?" the driver asked. It seemed queer for him to call me kid. He didn't look over twenty-two and I was sixteen.

"I'm Harry Maslow," I said.

"I'm Joe Stuckey," he said. "Now why don't you take off your shoes, and I'll rev up that heater for you and you can dry your feet. Wet feet's a sure way to get the virus."

I didn't feel much like taking my shoes off, but I did. I looked the driver over a bit while I was doing it. He didn't have much of any chin, but he was trying to grow a beard. He was really pretty homely, with that ring of black whiskers under his mouth. His complexion was awful, and his hair hung down over his ears.

"Where you been?" he asked me, when I got my shoes off, and my long feet stashed under the heater.

"I was at a camp," I said. "A church camp. I have a nice girl, and I dated her last night at this church camp." I didn't know how much else to tell him yet. One had to think of his witness, of course, all the time, but I wasn't warm to this boy yet. I sure couldn't tell him anything he'd understand about that great sermon I heard. The evangelist preached about keeping oneself unspotted from the world. It was tremendous.

"So if she's such a great girl, why you going home?" the driver asked.

"I got a Sunday school class in the morning," I said. "Ten-year-old boys. I got to get ready a lesson."

"Nawww!" the driver said. "You're a Sunday school

teacher. Why'd I have to go pick up a Sunday school teacher?"

His voice was real screechy, and when he said the word "teacher" the second time, it cracked. He was grinning. What a row of bad teeth! This boy was a real pain to look at.

"I'm death on 'em," he said, showing his bad teeth. "I hate 'em."

I was a little nervous. He was driving about fifty. There was no back door out of this one. Joe Stuckey and I were going to be together for a while, and he said he didn't like Sunday school teachers. Also I wasn't sure I liked him.

He winked at me. "I broke a couple Sunday school teachers' hearts," he said. "I'm bad. See if you can guess where I'm coming from."

That was too hard. On this highway, he could be coming from almost anywhere east or south. I shook my head. That let some more water run off my hair down my neck.

"I'm coming from Wheeling," he said. "I took my wife and my little boy back to her folks. She was getting lonesome. She thinks she's going to be there a couple weeks, and then I'm going back to get her and Lenny. Only thing is, I'm not going back." He chuckled.

I stared at him. "You're not going back?"

"No, sir. I'm getting lost in the big wicked city. I'm going to run around all I like, and no bossy little woman to tell me when I got to be in at night. Only thing I'm sorry about is my boy. He's as mean as a striped snake, and I'm going to miss him. But I'm not going to miss that bossing. Uh-uh." He ran his tongue over his lips and rolled his eyes.

He made me sick at my stomach.

Actually, I wanted to get out right there. Maybe leave a Gospel of John on the seat and scram. But there was no leaving, with him gunning down the slick highway at fifty per.

About this time he takes out a skinny cigar and bites at one end. Then he lights it with the dashboard lighter. To myself I groan, because I never did like cigar smoke. I figured I was going to get smoked up good like a Virginia ham, and nothing in the world to do about it.

"I got only one," he said, sort of apologizing.

"I don't smoke," I told him, trying to say it so he'd get the idea I didn't want to *be* smoked, either.

He didn't catch on. Pretty soon, the blue cloud settled around my head and shoulders, so I opened my side window. I didn't care if it rained in.

Then it comes to me like a shock. This is it, boy. If you ever saw it. This is the *world*. The mean, ugly wicked world. This is what the Christian has got to watch out for, or he takes on spots. He goes rotten like the good apple in the bad barrel. I decided to myself that I was going to be careful. This Joe Stuckey was contagious.

"So you like that little boy," I said. "Maybe he's going to miss his daddy." I didn't really believe that, but I figured I had to say something. Homes shouldn't break up this way.

Joe Stuckey poked his cigar into the dashboard ashtray and wagged his head. "Don't you go softening me up, teacher," he said. "I got my mind made up, and it wasn't easy. Nothing's going to change it now."

I looked away. I couldn't stand that grin and those awful teeth. I'd about used up all the grace I had. I'd be sure to leave a Gospel of John on the seat. That would take care of things.

We were coming to a city-limit sign. *Fordham. Population* 14,300. About a thousand feet ahead there was a traffic light. Stuckey eased up a little on the gas feed. That light was green, but it wasn't going to stay green long enough.

I started pulling on my shoes. If it looked like a real good corner ... well you just couldn't tell.

Joe eyed me real suspiciously. "What you doing?" he asked.

"I think my feet are dry," I said. "Besides I don't want to go forgetting my shoes."

"You're not leaving me now, are you?" Joe said. I ran a finger down the part in my sopping hair. I thought a little. This guy was a real sad sack. One minute he's telling me he hates Sunday school teachers, and the next he sounds sorry to see me putting on my shoes.

"I don't know," I said. "If this is a real good corner." But by this time I could see that the light didn't mark an intersection. A street came in from the right. It didn't go through. Of course, there would be lots of intersections in a town of 14,000.

We waited at the light. The red was reflected on the shiny wet pavement.

"I been looking for someone to talk to," Joe said while we waited. "It's a funny thing, all my life I been mixed up with people who like to talk, nothing else. My bossy wife, her bossy mother, the guys at the station where I work, everybody. Nobody wants to listen. You got two ears. Maybe you know how to listen." He had put the cigar back in his mouth and was chewing the end.

I didn't say anything. I was waiting for him to start choking me with that cigar smoke.

We came to another traffic light, but he had the green here, so he gunned on through, not giving me a chance to make my move.

In fact, when we got through the intersection, he swerved from the outside lane to the inside lane, to get around a slow car that had come from the right.

He shouldn't have done that.

That ugly sound of metal gouging metal

There wasn't any honking, just that ugly noise of metal gouging metal. Shrill, grating, nasty.

There'd been a car coming in that inner lane behind us in the blind spot where the inside rear view mirror doesn't help you any. Both cars had been trying to use a stretch of wet road by the center line.

Joe Stuckey was white-faced. His black beard looked like false whiskers, pasted on. Maybe he was scared, but he was plenty mad, too.

He rolled down his window. The driver from the other car got out and came up. He was about forty-five in a suit. His car was a new Pontiac.

"Stupe!" Joe said real loud. "You toting a pig through that light? I own a piece of this road just like you. What a fathead idea, sneaking up behind me."

The other driver didn't say anything. His mouth was working around as if he was chewing some words he couldn't get out. I could understand his trouble. This was Joe's fault. That was plain as the fender lying back on the pavement. Lots of people would have owned up and had it over with.

The other driver had big eyes and high cheekbones. He managed to say something finally. "Witnesses," he said. "Witnesses. I have witnesses. People on the corner."

Joe spit out the window on the pavement. I couldn't see, but I figured he'd just missed the other driver's feet. "You can junk all that," he said. "I got a witness too." He hooked a finger in my direction.

The other driver stared at me. He looked hurt. I was ready to set both of them straight, when the man in the window turned on his heel. "Stay here. The police. I'll call them."

He left, and we both watched him go into the drugstore on the corner. As soon as he was out of sight, Joe started the car. His mouth was set.

"Hey," I shouted, "don't be a fool. He's got your license number. There are fifty people around."

The car had stalled, and in the silence, Joe Stuckey looked at me. "That's sense," he said. "But you going to be my witness?"

141

I groaned. This was it, okay. Roll around in the barrel with a rotten apple, and this is what happens.

"Don't ask me that," I said. "I got to be honest. Besides, there are fifty people outside who saw what happened." By this time the traffic was tied up a mile behind the intersection, and a crowd was hunching up close.

I was lacing my shoes.

Pretty soon the police came. A couple of patrolmen walked around looking at the skid marks on the wet pavement. I figured that was all the evidence they needed. Everything was written there, like on a blackboard. I'd stick around maybe a minute more, and be sure the right guy took the rap. I had eighty miles to go before I was home.

We both got out of the car. I took a Gospel of John from my shirt pocket and left it on the seat.

The police were busy talking with the other driver. They'd be with us in a couple seconds.

"Look," Joe said to me. "Maybe you aren't going to be my witness, but I need you to stick around; you see, I got nobody." His little eyes were like a puppy's when he thinks maybe you're going to give it a boot down the stairs.

I didn't say anything. What could I say to him? I had eighty miles to go, and a Sunday school lesson to get ready.

The police came over. They started asking questions. They didn't give Joe much chance to argue. The case was settled. They asked about insurance.

Joe shrugged. "Sure, what do you think? Let me check my glove compartment." He walked back to the car. I followed him because I was going to get my duffel bag out of the back seat.

He jumped into the front seat and began pawing through the glove compartment. He was talking under his breath. I didn't try to hear what he was saying.

I opened the back door.

Joe spoke up. He let out a string of profanity. Then, "I haven't got any insurance. Haven't had any for six months. I'll give the stupes my name and address. They can find out for themselves." He pulled a paper from the glove compartment.

Then he caught sight of the Gospel I had left on the seat. He picked it up and read the title. He looked back at me.

I had my duffel bag and was climbing out.

"Hey!" he screamed. "Wait. You leaving me?"

"I got another eighty miles to go, tonight . . ."

"What's this book you left?" he said, still screaming.

"That's for you. That's a Gospel of . . ."

Then he got foolish-mad. He took the little booklet and threw it at me. It hit me in the chest, but it didn't hurt any.

"Scram!" he said screechingly. "I don't want anything more to do with you. Go home to your Sunday school."

He hollered some other things after me, sort of crying, as I walked toward the next intersection, but I wasn't listening. Boy, talk about staying unspotted in the world. It took all a guy had, and maybe a little more.

It was still raining. I found a good spot by the traffic light and began to wait for another ride. I was a little hurt, the way he'd treated the Gospel of John.

But I guess you waste your time worrying about his kind.[1]

How will you handle it?

You may never have had exactly the kind of experience described by the fictitious Harry Maslow in this last chapter. Perhaps you are not quite as hung up as he was on "staying unspotted by the world." But where is the Christian who hasn't found himself saying that "I sure blew it with him" or "I wish I could have said something, but I just didn't know how to start"?

Following are some ideas (adapted from the pages of *Campus Life*) for "getting a start."

1. *Be sure Christ is really running your life.* Perhaps you're not witnessing because you don't have much to say about what Christ is doing in your life. If this is possibly your problem, stop right now and think about areas of your life you should give completely to Christ. What about the amount of time you spend in prayer and reading His Word? Knowing the faith and feeling the faith (living it as "something for real") are the two wings of your witnessing airplane. But the Word of God is the fuel. No fuel, no flight.

2. *Accept yourself, failures and all.* Don't wait until you feel you're "spiritual enough" to witness. To be filled with the Spirit is a great goal and ideal but you will never feel completely full day in and day out. Seek to communicate Christ anyway, and you will find that this just may be the one way to know more of the fullness of His Spirit.

3. *Don't be a victim of "scalp-think."* That is, don't look at people as potential scalps on your spiritual belt. This approach has probably done more to turn off non-Christians than anything else. They quickly detect an attitude that simply wants them to join another group or be added to another list of converts. Few people are interested in that. They've been sold to death in this high-powered age of hard sell. But what they may be interested in is the *real thing* concerning God. If you suspect you're guilty of scalp-think, confess it to God and ask Him to give you an attitude of "Christ-think" instead. The idea is that you don't want to take scalps, but you do want to share Christ.

4. *Realize your responsibility but relax.* No question about it, when it comes to knowing a vital life-changing experience in Christ, you and your fellow Christians are definitely outnumbered by a vast horde of unbelievers. This gives you an unlimited opportunity, but don't try to get everybody saved all at once. Relax and let the Holy Spirit work through you. How do you do that? Stay alert to the Holy Spirit and He will lead you to talk to the person He chooses at the time He wants you to.

You don't have to preach the entire plan of salvation every time you talk to a non-Christian. With most people this does more harm than good. You're right back to scalp-think again. But as you are alert to the Holy Spirit, talking to God and asking Him for opportunities and openings, you will get them. You have God's Word on it.

Besides the basic portions of Scripture that you should know in order to explain Christianity to interested people (review chapter 9), make these thoughts from God's Word part of your witnessing plans:

"Always be joyful. Always keep on praying. Always be thankful no matter what happens, for that is God's will for you who belong to Christ Jesus. Do not smother the Holy Spirit" (1 Thess. 5:16-19, LNT).

Be confident. God has promised He will answer your prayers.

"And we are sure of this, that He will listen to us whenever we ask Him for anything in line with His will. And if we really know He is listening when we talk to Him and make our requests, then we can be sure that He will answer us" (1 John 5:14,15, LNT).

Live the life in order to win the right to be heard.

"Be their ideal; let them follow the way you teach and live; be a pattern for them in your love, your faith, and your clean thoughts" (1 Tim. 4:12, LNT).[2]

SOMEBODY LOVED a LOSER

"Never giving up on a loser" is a familiar plot. You see it in magazines, books, in newspapers, on TV and in the films . . .

Hopelessly awkward 6'8" freshman can't get out of his own way when he comes out for basketball practice. But patient coach keeps working with him. As a senior, he's all-American . . .

Shaky intern almost kills emergency heart attack victim, but chief surgeon catches wrong diagnosis in time. Instead of shipping erring intern back to male nurses' school, kindly chief surgeon helps him go on to become world-famous heart specialist . . .

Young teacher wants to quit because she can't handle her 4th grade class of incorrigible ghetto brats, but veteran principal talks her out of it and helps her go on to become a master teacher . . .

You can find "somebody loved a loser" stories in the Bible too. In fact, the entire Bible is a story of

147

how Somebody loved a loser. The world was a loser and God so loved the world that He gave His only Son . . .

Jesus must have had plenty of moments when He may have thought it was time to send some of the disciples back to mending their nets. And then there is the story of Barnabas, living proof that nice guys *can* finish first. Because Barnabas was willing to give a loser named John Mark a second chance the early church gained one of its strongest workers and the Bible has the Gospel of Mark as well.

You run across Barnabas in the book of Acts. A native of the island of Cyprus, he was a Jew by birth. In fact, he was a Levite, a descendant of the Jewish tribe of Levi, whose original assignment in the days of Moses was to preserve the law of Jehovah and to assist in maintaining the tabernacle.

You might say Barnabas came from a "fine old Jewish family" and was something of a blue blood. His original name was Joseph, but after joining the Christian ranks he was named Barnabas, meaning, "son of encouragement." It seemed Barnabas was a man people liked to have around.

A major reason people liked to have him around seems to be that he was willing to go out on a limb for others. For example, when his fellow Christians were going hungry, Barnabas sold a field he owned and put the money in the "deacon's fund." (See Acts 4:37.)

Barnabas not only risked his pocketbook, but he risked his reputation, even his personal safety. Paul —originally a vicious persecutor of the Christian church—was converted on the road to Damascus, but a lot of Christians wouldn't believe he had really changed. When he tried to join their ranks they shunned him in fear or contempt but Barnabas stepped in and introduced Paul to the apostles at Jerusalem and vouched for the genuineness of his conversion. That was all they needed. Their distrust of Paul turned into immediate acceptance. (See Acts 9:26-28.)

When large numbers of Gentiles began turning to Christ, Barnabas went up to Antioch and was a tremendous source of encouragement and spiritual strength. "Barnabas was a kindly person, full of the Holy Spirit and strong in faith. As a result large numbers of people were added to the Lord" (Acts 11:24, LNT).

Barnabas saw tremendous potential in the congregation at Antioch, a huge and beautiful city, often called the capital of the eastern part of the Roman Empire. So Barnabas invited Paul to team up with him and for a year they taught a large group of converts at Antioch. Barnabas and Paul made such a good team that, one day as prophets and teachers of the church were praying and fasting, the Holy Spirit said, "Dedicate Barnabas and Paul for a special job I have for them" (Acts 13:2, LNT).

That "special job" turned out to be the first missionary expedition sent out by the first century church. As they planned, prayed and fasted in preparation for the trip, Barnabas and Paul decided to take along an assistant—Barnabas' young cousin, John Mark. John Mark's home was Jerusalem, but while on a business trip to Jerusalem Paul and Barnabas had invited John Mark to return to Antioch and he had agreed (see Acts 12:25).

You could call John Mark one of the first "kids who was raised in the church." John Mark's mother's home was actually a center of the Jerusalem church. It was in her house that the disciples prayed for Peter when the court freed him from prison (see Acts 12:12, *LNT*). Disciples and apostles were frequent guests in Mark's home and he must have known many of them as personal friends. It is quite possible that as a young boy he had seen Jesus teaching near the Temple. Perhaps he had even heard Jesus speak in his own home.

So, from his earliest years, John Mark had been involved in the life of the church. He was well acquainted with the Gospel—the Good News—and had witnessed its power. It was no surprise then that Barnabas, coleader of this first missionary team, suggested that Mark go along as an assistant.

Barnabas, Paul and Mark sailed for Cyprus, and when they arrived they preached from town to town across the entire island. For Barnabas it was a dream fulfilled. Cyprus was his home and these were his own people hearing the Gospel for the first time. Their preaching communicated. When they left Cyprus even the governor had believed in Christ—and their trip wasn't even half over!

Barnabas and Paul were excited and eager to push on, but apparently Mark wasn't. When the party landed at the town of Perga in Turkey Mark left them to return home (see Acts 13:13).

Scripture doesn't spell out why Mark deserted Barnabas and Paul. He might have been ill. Perhaps he got worried about his mother, a widow living alone in Jerusalem. Another guess is that Mark might have started to resent Paul, who seemed to assume more and more leadership as the tour progressed. After all, Mark's cousin Barnabas had started out as coleader.

Did Mark have the "integration blues"?

A strong possibility is that Mark began to have doubts about sharing the Gospel with Gentiles. Paul and Barnabas were eagerly preaching the message of Christ to Jews and Greeks alike. Remember, Mark had been born and reared a Jew. His own church in Jerusalem was made up of practically all Jewish converts. Perhaps Mark felt the way many Jewish Christians felt at that time: "The Gospel is for us and not Gentiles because Gentiles have never been God's chosen people."

Paul and Barnabas finished their tour without Mark, returned home and reported that God had ". . . opened the door of faith to the Gentiles too" (Acts 14:27, LNT). Not long after, Paul suggested to Barnabas that they make a second journey to visit cities where they had started new churches and see how the new converts were doing. Apparently Mark was still living in Antioch because Barnabas suggested taking him along again. If you wanted to put Paul's reaction to that suggestion in modern vernacular, it might have gone something like this: "Take Mark? No way! The kid copped out on us once and our work is too important to have it happen again" (see Acts 15:38).

You can't blame Paul too much for feeling Mark was unreliable. Paul didn't want anyone along who wasn't prepared to finish the job and fulfill his commitments. Perhaps Paul saw Mark's first desertion as a serious breach of the faith. There could be no compromise on giving him another chance without more proof that he was now stable and trustworthy.

Paul's attitude put Barnabas in a tight spot. If he insisted on taking Mark, he risked offending Paul. They might even end up in a split. If they did split up it might look bad to the new churches they had started. How would they explain their lack of Christian unity? The whole thing could get sticky.

On the other hand, if Barnabas agreed with Paul, it could be more than Mark could handle emotionally. Obviously, Mark hadn't been quite ready the first time, but now it seems he was willing to go again. It took a certain amount of courage and conviction to try to make a comeback in the very job where he had failed. Mark might have real potential. How could Barnabas turn him down at this crucial point in his life?

Should Barnabas risk it with a loser?

Barnabas must have considered his possibilities. For example, Barnabas could agree with Paul. After all, a common attitude has always been, "Don't stick your neck out for somebody else." Why take a risk if there's nothing in it for you? Paul was obviously the real leader of the missionary forces by now and Barnabas could simply say,

"I'm under orders, Mark. I'm sorry, but you can't go along."

Besides, how could Barnabas disagree with Paul? Their work was crucial. Christ Himself had commissioned his followers to spread the Word everywhere (see Acts 1:8). Paul was probably right in saying they couldn't risk taking along someone who had failed them once and could quite possibly fail them again. Was Barnabas' friendship for Mark worth jeopardizing the work of the young church, which was just getting started?

But suppose Barnabas did want to disagree? Perhaps he could go over Paul's head and rally support from other leaders in the church. Maybe they could all pressure Paul into letting Mark go along. Paul was an important man, true, but he wasn't the whole show.

Barnabas might have tried this, but it's the kind of solution that appeals to a particular personality type and Barnabas wasn't that type. Pressuring Paul, going behind his back or over his head, this just wasn't for a man like Barnabas.

Well, how about a compromise? Barnabas could try to avoid the issue by making other arrangements for John Mark, an easier assignment in the Antioch area, perhaps, to give him some seasoning before he tried the missionary trail again. This solution certainly must have had its attractions for Barnabas. Even though he recommended Mark for a second missionary tour, Barnabas must have had a few reservations about how the young man might perform. Maybe he wasn't ready.

But then Barnabas would have to answer other

difficult questions. Would Mark ever grow as a person if he were not given a chance to redeem himself? Apparently Mark wanted to go on this tour quite badly. It took a certain amount of courage and humility to be willing to volunteer and ask for a second chance.

Barnabas' decision is found in Acts 15:39-41. He stuck with this proposal and the disagreement between him and Paul ". . . was so sharp that they separated. Barnabas took Mark with him and sailed for Cyprus, while Paul chose Silas and, with the blessing of the believers, left for Syria and Cilicia, to encourage the churches there" (*LNT*).

Barnabas took a double risk. He broke up an effective relationship with the greatest leader the young church had; he took a chance on an unproven failure.

So what happened? Did Barnabas sail into oblivion? The Bible doesn't say, directly, but it almost seems as though Luke disapproved of Barnabas' choice. Note that he says Paul and Silas left with ". . . the blessing of the believers" (Acts 15:41, *LNT*). Barnabas and Mark simply left, and Luke doesn't go on to report what happened to them.

But other clues tell you that Barnabas' double risk paid off. Mark apparently became an effective and useful servant of Christ in the early church. Tradition has it that he spent a great deal of his time assisting the apostle Peter. The New Testament contains the Gospel he wrote. And—most interesting of all—when Paul wrote to Timothy from his prison cell in Rome—he said, "Bring Mark with you when you come" (2 Tim. 4:11, *LNT*).

Didn't Paul believe in loving losers?

It seems that Paul eventually gave Mark a second chance, too. In the disagreement with Barnabas, Paul sounds like the legalistic unrelenting commanding officer who will tolerate no traitors in the ranks. But who is to say just how Paul felt? Maybe he had just as much compassion for Mark as Barnabas did, but the weight of responsibility as leader forced him to say no in this case.

Sometimes God gives us different roles to play in different situations. To call Paul unloving and unforgiving is too simple. We don't have all the facts. Had you been Paul, you may have voted to leave Mark home, too, even though it appears that all Mark needed was someone to believe in him.

There is story after story just like Mark's. People can and do succeed when somebody is willing to believe in them and give them a chance. In fact, to treat the other guy in a way that says, "I really believe in you as a person" is just plain sound psychology and good common sense if you want to have friends.

Look at it this way. You can be a helper or someone who needs help. The world breaks nicely into groups of either one. Because most people are looking for help, chances are you will have more friends and find more success if you choose to be a helper. How do you do that? Here are a few pointers:

1. *Be real—someone others can trust.* In short, don't be a phony. There are two places to be real. When you are with other people and when you're

not. Most of us realize that we shouldn't talk behind others' backs but keep in mind that it's important how you talk to people's faces, and that brings up point two . . .

2. *Be open and honest.* Don't say one thing with your lips and another with your eyes and your facial expression. So many relationships in life are between people who are playing games with one another. It is very difficult to know when one person is being put down and someone else is being put on and still someone else is being put out or off. Some people are real pros at this. Seek to be an amateur.

3. *Try to let yourself go.* That is, if you feel warm or friendly or complimentary toward somebody, be that way. One of the hardest things for a lot of us is to pay a compliment. It just isn't cool. Somebody might think we're corny or trying to chalk up brownie points on the social scoreboard.

But unless you can be yourself, you will never let the other person be himself. In other words, don't build relationships with others on the basis of expecting them to shape up to fit your charming personality. Maybe you are not really that charming.

4. *So, try to see things from the other person's point of view.* You can't do this completely, of course, but for openers, try saying, "Now, let's see, if I were (Betty, John or Alice or Mark, etc., etc.) how would I feel about this?" If you start thinking this way at least two things happen: You get off dead center (yourself); you start reaching out to others, which is the whole idea behind trying to be a helper—not helpless.

5. Right along with seeing things from the other fellow's viewpont, *stop playing the evaluation game*. The Bible is hard on people who do. "Don't criticize, and then you won't be criticized! For others will treat you as you treat them. And why worry about a speck in the eye of a brother when you have a board in your own?" (See Matt. 7:1-3, *LNT*.)

Most people are sick unto death of being judged, rated, classified, graded, stamped (and in some cases, shipped). So take your conversational temperature. The more often you make judgmental remarks the colder you are going to seem to other people.

6. *Finally, if you have to label people, call them "in process,"* not "hopeless," "cop-out," "lazy," etc. One of the easiest things in the world is to pigeon-hole somebody, box him in neatly in your mind. Label him "undependable" or "can't be trusted." Label her "fast" or "supermouth." After all, life isn't so threatening if you can keep people boxed in.

In the summer of 1970, the United States Army had several hundred tons of nerve gas that was a real problem so they boxed it up in concrete vaults and sent it 16,000 feet to Davy Jones's locker. Psychologically speaking, you can do the same with people. You can put them in vaults (certain prejudiced compartments of your mind) and never let them out. They can be at the bottom of the ocean for all the difference your relationship to them makes. They're never going to grow or change, or even be aware that they could be anything different, because you won't let them.

To put it another way, do you see people as "somebody with a past," or do you see them as "somebody with a future"?

All of the pointers listed above will help you be a helper; part of the solution, not the problem. Some people may even succeed or improve because of how you treat them. Like John Mark, they may come through because you believe in them. That's good psychology.[1]

But what if you believe in someone, give him a second chance, maybe even a third, and he fails? Let's face it. There will be a lot more people who fail than who make it. There will be some people who never do change one millimeter no matter how you treat them.

Then you have a little different ball game. Then, the question is, can you keep right on believing and giving people another chance and another and another? According to Christ, that's good Christianity. (See excerpt from *Tough Love*, Bill Milliken's excellent book on Young Life work in the inner city, p. 159.)

Barnabas didn't give Mark another chance because he'd read a first century version of *How to Win Friends and Influence Missionary Candidates*. Instead, Barnabas was putting into action what Jesus once told His disciples when they asked Him about giving people another chance. Was seven times enough? "No!" Jesus replied. "Seventy times seven!" (See Matt. 18:21,22.)

Barnabas knew somebody had to love the losers. Perhaps Barnabas remembered that God had loved him, and he had been a loser, too. When it comes

Duke: "What's wrong, Bill? Can't I fail anymore?"

I was learning lessons, too, through Duke. Sometimes it was my own insecurity that demanded Duke make it, because I wanted to have him as a good example of what we're accomplishing in the inner city. He got on me once about that. I wanted him to speak at some meeting, and he was messing up so badly, that he felt he couldn't talk about Christ. In my disappointment I told him he would have to speak anyway, which of course would have been phony.

Duke came back at me with, "What's wrong, Bill? Can't I fail anymore?"

He was absolutely right, and I knew it. My own sinful self had been demanding recognition because I was embarrassed about admitting to that suburban church that my man was messing up and couldn't talk that week.

Duke had really learned to ask hard questions. "When I'm failing, you just don't like me, do you, Bill?"

He was hitting me where it hurt. I said, "Duke, I'm sorry. You hit it on the head—I haven't given you the freedom of failure."

I was worthless at staff meeting that night. I kept thinking, "Milliken, you've got to love people who fail. You've got to stay with them when they're messing up. You can't hit them when they're down."

So often we just don't let people fail. We've got to experience failure before we can really know how to succeed. If we could just know this and accept it and work at it! The whole Christian church needs to work at it. Our fear of failure is what makes us build up legalism.

—From *Tough Love*, by Bill Milliken,
Young Life Worker on New York's lower East Side.[1]

ANOTHER CHANCE
ANOTHER CHANCE
ANOTHER CHANCE
ANOTHER CHANCE
ANOTHER CHANCE

How often should I forgive my brother?

Acts 15:39

to losers, you have a simple choice: Love 'em or leave 'em.

How will you handle it?

Giving others a second chance sounds loving and idealistic, but do you have the attitude to do it? Are you willing to let God give you this attitude? The following quiz asks hard questions; God's Word offers answers, but they aren't pat solutions.

1. How do you see other people? That is, do you realize that every person has worth and dignity because God made him?

". . . be kind to each other, tenderhearted, forgiving one another, just as God has forgiven you because you belong to Christ" (Eph. 4:32, *LNT*).

* * * * * *

2. Do you consciously try to treat other people as though they are worth something, or do you subtly cut them down by the way you talk and act?

"Since you have been chosen by God who has given you this new kind of life, and because of His deep love and concern for you, you should practice tenderhearted mercy and kindness to others" (Col. 3:12, *LNT*).

* * * * * *

3. Are you willing to let others be themselves or do you feel you are God's associate, who is commissioned to "shape them up"?

"Your heavenly Father will forgive you if you forgive those who sin against you; but if *you* refuse to forgive *them, He* will not forgive *you*" (Matt. 6:14,15, *LNT*).

* * * * * *

Think of a person or persons who need to get a second chance — *from you*. Maybe they need a lot of second chances, almost every day. You probably won't have to go very far from home to find people who need a second chance. Maybe you won't have to leave home at all . . .

WHaT DoeS YOUR CHURCH Do FOR YOU?

"What does my church do for me? Why, nothing."

"It's irrelevant, not willing to face the real issues, hopelessly behind the times . . ."

"The church has blown it, John Lennon was right. It's only a matter of time until Christianity dies out . . ."

Hmmmm . . . this seems to be where we came in with this book. Is our last "profile of faith" going to have us go out the same way?

It would be easy to do just that. Nothing is easier than criticizing, especially chopping the church.

But to paraphrase the old saying, "Christianity hasn't been tried and found to be a failure. Christianity has been found difficult and people have decided to quit trying."

And your reply might be, "That's not quite it. You see I *want* to try Christ, but I'm not sure my church does. At least, they don't seem to want to try to do things that are meaningful to me as far as God and Jesus Christ are concerned."

162

163

164

Perhaps the following "Open Letter to God" written by a young person expresses your feelings, or the feelings of some people you may know . . .

* * * * * *

"Let me be blunt. . . . This turmoil has been festering and growing ever since my faith in You came to be personal rather than borrowed. I'm torn between being a Christian on one hand, and a churchman on the other . . .

"First of all, I know what life as your friend can be like . . . you're real, you're alive, you're with me, *I know that.*

"The hitch comes in that institution you ordained long ago. I know countless others have complained about the church and cursed it, and shot it full of holes. I don't know their motives but I do know that mine is one of loving concern. As I read Acts and the Letters of Paul, I can see what you really wanted from the church, and the ideas were great. I feel exhilarated when I think of what the church could be if we stuck to your directions. But I feel disgusted when I look and see what has evolved from that first perfect blueprint.

"Right now I find the church stifling my friendship with you. Those services three times a week tend to bore me rather than stimulate my thinking. Worst of all, most ideas for change meet with hard-nose disapproval from the stalwarts who run the institution."[1]

* * * * * *

"What does your church do for you?" is a very relevant question today. If your church does a lot for you then you will want to know how to answer its critics. If your church isn't doing much for you, it's time to try to figure out why.

The writer of the open letter to God puts his finger on what he feels are many weak spots in his church. He sees the book of Acts and Paul's letters

165

as a perfect blueprint of what God wants from the church. Interestingly enough, however, a lot of Paul's letters were written to young churches just a few years removed from the very event of Christ's death and Resurrection *who were already experiencing "problems."* They were already suffering from hardening of the organizational arteries.

But it's a funny thing . . . Paul wrote lots of letters to lots of churches with problems but he never talked about the church being dead. He never proclaimed that Christianity had failed. He didn't point to a lack of involvement in social issues. Instead, Paul had the disturbing habit of talking about Christ and the spiritual condition of the *church members.*

The early church had its "gaps," too

Paul didn't spend a lot of time developing critiques of church procedures or the sociological reasons behind the generation gap. Yes, there was a generation gap in the first century church. Paul's two letters to his young protégé Timothy tell you a lot about that gap, whether you just read the lines or whether you read between them.

Paul had met Timothy in Lystra while on his second missionary tour. Paul was impressed with the young man and all of the good reports people gave of him. He offered Timothy a job—no pay but an unlimited future—as part of his missionary team. Timothy accepted, became Paul's understudy and accompanied him on the rest of his second missionary journey as well as his third.

Paul and Timothy made a good team, but eventually they had to split up. Paul wound up in a prison cell in Rome. Timothy had been sent to Ephesus, hundreds of miles away, on special assignment to try to keep the churches in that area going and growing. It was no small task. Already, doctrinal errors were creeping in. People were rewriting the Gospel a little, some out of ignorance, and some deliberately because their own revisions suited them better. Timothy went to Ephesus to direct, organize and supervise the work of the churches—a job calling for tact, drive, courage and skill.

Paul thought often about Timothy and his difficult and demanding assignment. He decided to write to him, to give him encouragement, advice and ideas for serving Christ and building His church. If you bother to read both of Paul's letters to Timothy, you will quickly detect the personal pep-talk tone. And you will also see that while Paul believed in giving his friend a pep talk he also knew that the only real source of help and strength for him was Jesus Christ. For example, in 2 Timothy 2:3-5, Paul talks about what it takes to live the Christian life and serve in the church:

"Take your share of suffering as a good soldier of Jesus Christ, just as I do. And as Christ's soldier do not let yourself become tied up in worldly affairs, for then you cannot satisfy the one who has enlisted you in his army. Follow the Lord's rules for doing His work, just as an athlete either follows the rules or is disqualified and wins no prize" (2 Tim. 2:3-5, *LNT*).

Paul often used references to soldiers and athletes in his writings. He was never in the army, and as far as anyone can tell, was strictly a spectator when it came to sports. But Paul recognized a quality in the life of the soldier and the athlete that is absolutely vital for the Christian. That quality is *discipline*—something that seems to be in short supply these days in the church. Could that be one reason why a lot of people aren't happy with the church? Young people are quite convinced that the adults aren't disciplined and so they call them hypocrites. On the other side of the generation gap, the adults are equally convinced that the young people aren't disciplined and they call them irresponsible.

Perhaps the church is reaping what it sowed. Today the church has a generation that is long on griping and short on coming to grips with what the Bible really has to say, because it has watched an older generation that has never really come to grips with the Bible either.

Writing in *Eternity* magazine, Joseph Bayly sends the following "word to the now generation":

"We older people are a mess.

"But what hurts the most is this: So are you. And I suspect that's why you're so bitter about us. You hate to see the mess perpetuated in yourselves. You see your generation going down the same hypocritical path.

"You can reject our hair styles. Our conformity, our ticky-tacky houses, crummy bourgeois tendencies, moral absolutes, music.

"Deep down, don't you wish you could reject our materialism as well, that 13 billion-dollar-a-year slice you personally spend? The soft living, plush houses, fast cars you like as much as we do?

"But that would involve sacrifice, poverty, which are things to sing about, not things to do.

"Empty words.

"Do as I sing, not as I do.

"We're fakey, but so are you. You say everything's relative, you want us to look at you in shades of gray—but then you judge us by our own absolute standard of black and white.

"Honesty is your prime virtue, if we hear you right. Then why all the cheating and shoplifting?

"You don't mean honesty like that? You mean frankness, openness about sex and morals, no pretense?

". . . Neither of us is happy, your generation or mine. No hypocrite ever is. The difference is that we're 20 years closer to the end of the game than you."[2]

And so the generation gap widens (or is it the myths that cause the "gap" that are getting bigger?).

People on both sides of the gap tend to play a game called "psychological sniper." They keep pushing their own ideas of style, taste—the prejudices of their particular subculture, be it prethirty or postthirty. Many demand change "by the other generation." Few—on either side of the gap—exhibit much discipline.

But according to Paul, discipline is part of being a Christian. Living the Christian life means following the rules and staying in spiritual shape. That's why Paul says, "Follow the Lord's rules for doing His work, just as an athlete either follows the rules or is disqualified . . ." (2 Tim. 2:5, *LNT*).

Many a gifted athlete has wound up a loser and has even failed to make the first team because he neglected this basic rule. To excel in any sport—to even make the team—you have to train, and train, and train some more.

Could Allen's Ten Commandments help?

George Allen, professional football coach who brought the Los Angeles Rams from the ranks of the also-rans to a winning team in the late 1960's, lives by a code that people call "Allen's Ten Commandments."

Allen's commandments—which have striking application to serious Christian living—are these:

1. *Football comes first.* During the N.F.L. season, Allen tells his players that football comes ahead of everything else, even family and church.

2. *The greatest feeling in life is to take an ordinary job and accomplish something with it.* Allen believes that even the most ordinary job can give its doer the joy of accomplishment.

3. *If you can accept defeat and open your pay envelope without feeling guilty, then you are stealing.* According to Allen the average N.F.L. player makes a sizable salary, but he "can't think of a thing this money will buy that a loser could enjoy. As far as I'm concerned, life without victories is like being in prison."

4. *Everyone, the head coach especially, must give 110%.* Allen believes that the average American may think he is a hard worker, but most people are operating on less than half steam. "They never get above 50% although they think of themselves as 90% producers," says Allen. "Therefore, to get 100%, you must aim for 110%."

5. *Leisure time is that five or six hours when you sleep at night.* Allen doesn't think people should work all the time. Everybody deserves some leisure and the early morning hours are best. He believes that "you can combine two good things at once, sleep and leisure."

6. *No detail is too small. No task is too small or too big.* Allen believes that winning is the science of being

totally prepared and he defines preparation in three words: "Leave nothing undone." He believes the difference between success and failure is so small that it can't be perceived by most people.

"A loser is a man who is unprepared and doesn't know he's unprepared," says Allen. "A winner is a man who consciously does everything he can think of to prepare himself as completely as possible."

7. *You must accomplish things in life, otherwise you are like the paper on the wall.* "The achiever," says Allen, "is the only individual who is truly alive. I see no difference between a chair and the man who sits in the chair if he is not accomplishing.

"Performance is the only thing that counts. Succeeding—winning—is the only true measure of a player and, therefore, everything I do, if it makes winning more likely, is fun. I believe that nothing is impossible to those that are willing to pay the price, and I believe that paying the price is in itself an enjoyable part of winning."

8. *A person without problems is dead.*

Allen believes that everybody has problems but "the successful person solves his." He acknowledges them, works on them and solves them. He is not disturbed when another day brings another kind of problem. That is exactly what he expects to come. He just goes to work on it.

9. *We win and lose as a team.*

"In the years when the Rams were losing," says Allen, "they tended to think of themselves as individuals . . . when individuals can't take pride in their team, they can sustain themselves by thinking of their individual greatness. But the fact is that football is a team game. If the team fails, everybody fails. If the team wins, everybody is a success."

10. *My prayer is that each man will be allowed to play to the best of his ability.*

"The individual who uses the ability he was given

when he was put on this earth—who works to the very limit of that ability—is doing what the Lord intended him to do. This is what life is all about. This is my religion."[3]

* * * * * *

Do George Allen's Ten Commandments sound a bit stiff? Would applying them to the Christian life turn you into a Pharisee and a legalist? Let's see what they would look like, "revisited."

1. *Jesus Christ comes first.*

The competition in life is tough. If you want to succeed in Christian living you have to put Christ ahead of everything and everyone else. That's what Jesus meant when He said, "Anyone who wants to be My follower must love Me far more than his own father, mother, wife, children, brothers, or sisters—yes, more than his own life—otherwise he cannot be My disciple. And no one can be My disciple who does not carry his own cross and follow Me" (Luke 14:26,27, *LNT*).

2. *The greatest feeling in life is to know that no matter how ordinary your job, as a Christian you can accomplish something for God.*

A lot of jobs in the church are quite ordinary. It's easy to want to junk the routine matters and think about saving the whole world. But without the routine, few teams or organizations will succeed, and the church is certainly no exception. The Scriptures say that in everything you do, do it heartily as unto the Lord, and you will find that sense of accomplishment.

3. *If you can continue to accept defeat and not have it bother you enough to want to change, perhaps you are guilty of stealing God's grace.*

If you can continue to accept a mediocre Christian existence and never seek to do anything about the spiritual defeats you suffer, then perhaps you don't want to grow or change. Perhaps you are quite willing to let God promise you heaven because of His grace (His unmerited favor and mercy) but that grace doesn't make any difference in your life.

Dietrich Bonhoeffer, German theologian who was martyred by the Nazis in World War II, calls it "cheap grace." Cheap grace is what keeps many a church in the ranks of the losers. You can't win them all, but unless you win some you get the loser mentality and that can happen to the Christian just as easily as it can happen to the athlete.

4. *Everyone—from the pastor right on down— must give 110%.*

Most Christians say amen to this—especially about the pastor giving 110%. Many a church wants the pastor to give 210%, while a lot of the congregation comes up with anywhere from 20% to 30% to 40%. In fact, when it comes to money, few churches can say that their members are giving 10%!

If many Christians were honest, they would have to admit that as far as the church and Jesus Christ are concerned, they seldom give anywhere near 50% of their available time and energy to the work. But if a football player is supposed to aim for 110% to get 100%, where does that leave a Christian?

Romans 5:2 says that, ". . . because of our faith, He has brought us into this place of highest privilege where we now stand, and we confidently and joyfully look forward to actually becoming all that God has had in mind for us to be" (*LNT*).

Christians like that verse. It sounds very good. The one hitch is that you become what God has in mind for you to be only as you make yourself available and put yourself into it.

God has a lot of things in mind for a lot of Christians and all He's waiting for is some cooperation. God undoubtedly has a lot of things in mind for today's church and all He's waiting for are people (over and under thirty) who want to give 110%. (In fact, God could probably accomplish quite a bit if all the Christians started giving 75 and 80%.)

5. *Leisure time can be useful or deadly as far as the Christian life is concerned.*

Increasing leisure time may be just one of the big reasons why the church of the 1970's is having less and less impact on its society. Increased vacation time, more weekends with the camper or with the boat, shorter weekdays and longer TV nights— all help to suck the Christian farther and farther into the hedonistic honey-pot.

Paul may or may not have foreseen the four-day work week but he knew what he was talking about when he said, "Don't let the world around you squeeze you into its own mold, but let God remold your minds from within, so that you may prove in practice that the plan of God for you is good, meets all his demands and moves toward the goal of true maturity" (Rom. 12:2, Phillips).

A lot of Christians can quote that verse from memory but they don't realize that with every year, and with every increased fringe benefit, they get squeezed more and more into the mold of the world. Leisure time is turning them into putty. The mold is doing the rest.

6. *When it comes to sharing the Gospel and teaching God's Word, no detail is too small.* Every task, large and small, is vital.

If winning can be described in three words ("leave nothing undone"), the church might be able to describe the reason for a lot of its losses in four words: "We didn't do it." The typical approach to church activities is: "Mediocrity is good enough—the Lord understands and He will undertake." But that's the motto of Christian losers—people who are unprepared and either don't know it or don't care. A Christian winner is a person who consciously does everything he can to prepare himself in every way possible to do the job that God wants him to do.

Think of what it would mean if Christians would prepare themselves for worship on Sunday morning with prayer and a reading of a psalm. Think of what it would mean if Sunday school teachers would start preparing themselves before Saturday night (or early Sunday morning). Think of what it would mean if Sunday school students, young and old, would quit faking it and really get down to business with studying Scripture and putting it to work in daily experience. It boggles the mind!

7. *You must accomplish things in the Christian life; otherwise you are like a parasite—a Bible termite.*

No wonder so many Christians feel their Christian life is dead. Too many churches are filled with people who are overstuffed with Bible lessons and sermons. But they haven't put these lessons or sermons to work in their own lives, in their own families or in the world.

The trouble with the church is not so much that it is ingrown but that it lacks growth. If Christians would really start growing on all the food they are supposed to be eating, real accomplishment in outreach (and inreach) would have to happen.

8. *Christians without problems are contradictions.*

"Christ will solve all your problems" is a much misunderstood and misused propaganda line. The truth is that every Christian has problems. Every Christian is aware of his major problem, which is sin. That's why he came to Christ in the first place. And coming to Christ doesn't result in instant perfection, instant holiness, or instant filling of the Spirit.

Christianity is a walk, not a sojourn in the winner's circle. The realistic Christian acknowledges his problems and solves them in, through and with Jesus Christ. As Jesus said, "Live one day at a time" (Matt. 6:34, *LNT*).

9. *Christians win or lose as the body of Christ.*

Christians are all one body, baptized into one Spirit (1 Cor. 12:13), and *they win or lose together.* If Christians—all those who are believers in Christ—would realize this, perhaps their church would accomplish more for the Saviour.

Too many churches have their individual stars (that soloist with the beautiful voice . . . that preacher with the eloquent sermons . . . that youth

director with all the go-power . . . that Bible teacher with incredible knowledge), *but these churches
are* still *losing the game*. No church can win in the
long run by relying on a few individual stars any
more than a football team can win with a superstar
quarterback who has to throw pass after pass to re-
ceivers with iron fingers who couldn't catch a ball
with a cargo net.

10. *Every Christian should be allowed to play to
the best of his ability*.

Now, Paul would certainly agree with that. You
might say that was Paul's reason for writing some
fourteen books in the New Testament. Paul wrote
about special abilities in the church in Ephesians,
chapter 4: "Why is it that He gives us these special
abilities to do certain things best? It is that God's
people will be equipped to do better work for Him,
building up the church, the body of Christ, to a po-
sition of strength and maturity" (Eph. 4:12, *LNT*).

To the church at Colossae Paul wrote, "Remember what Christ taught and let His words
enrich your lives and make you wise. . . . And
whatever you do or say, let it be as a representative
of the Lord Jesus . . ." (Col. 3:16,17, *LNT*).

* * * * * *

So much for applying football discipline to the
church, but perhaps you're still wondering. Would
discipline really help solve the church's generation
gap, not to mention its performance gap and influence gap? What about all the irrelevance, the lack
of social concern and awareness, the funeral dirge
music, the anti-intellectual pat answers???

There certainly is a lot to criticize, isn't there?

Why, without even trying you could decide your church doesn't do *anything* for you.

And then you really are dead because the simple truth is that what your church does for you depends entirely on what you do for Christ. *You are His church.*

When all of the analyses and criticisms and surveys and diagnoses of the generation gap are in, there still will be only one answer. The Holy Spirit fills the generation gap. Does that sound like a pat answer? Well, have you ever thought that all the chatter about the church being irrelevant, old-fashioned and helplessly out of it, is getting to be something of a pat criticism?

When it comes to the church and the need for change, you have three choices:

You can decide that things are going fine the way they are and just sit tight for the Second Coming.

You can be part of the criticism syndrome. You can become proficient in tearing down an old, seemingly vulnerable, institution. The church is definitely part of the establishment (the system), and nothing makes a better target than *that*.

Or, you can be a builder. You can work for change and updating of methods and ideas. (Never fear, the Bible will adapt itself quite nicely to your genius. It has managed to keep up with human intellect for severmal thousand years.)

But a word or two of caution: If you are young (in your ideas or your age), be sure you are striving to please Christ and not your subculture. If you are older and more conservative in your stance, be sure that in your resistance to certain changes, you are trying to serve the Saviour and not calcium-encrusted tradition.

It may be disconcerting to some people, but God is not the sole possession of those under thirty or those over thirty. He is the God of Abraham, Isaac and Jacob. He is the God of Armstrong, Aldrin and Collins. He is Alpha and Omega—the first and the last. He is not limited to Bach, "Bringing in the Sheaves" or a hard-rock Mass.

God is in Christ reconciling the world to Himself. Through Christ He works where and when He pleases and in anyone who is willing to allow Him to work. God must be a bit weary of all the flap over the gap when there is such a horrendous salvation gulf in the world, but He's patient.

God's waiting . . . He's waiting for you to take your choice.

Steve made his choice. Here's what happened...

"The next morning after I said yes to Christ, I expected to wake up, sorta like heaven, you know. Trumpets were supposed to sound, and everything was going to be cool . . . no problem, no hang-ups. But it was the same world, the same difficulties — only now, I had somebody to help me and eventually I began to understand Christ's role.

"God's love sort of works through you, and when you're relating to Him, you do everything He wants you to do. It's not an easy life. For instance, I still have to work for just 'C's' in school. God doesn't use a cookie-cutter on us. He doesn't force each Christian to be identical. God just asks each of us to love.

179

THE WORLD
IS CHANGING...
WHAT ABOUT YOU??
2 TIMOTHY 2:4,5

"This past year, I was in a contemporary Christian music group, singing and playing drums. Some adults didn't like the style of our group's music—okay, so they don't like it but that's no reason to turn against them. We had to still love them. It's hard to do, and I admit that I don't love everybody, but I'm learning to let God's love work through me.

"A lot of times I wonder why God doesn't leave, like when I doubt. I can be just miserable for a couple of days, when I don't turn to Him with my problems. But no matter how bad things get, He always pulls me back. I can't say how much it helps when I turn to Him and find the peace and joy He wants me to have. I guess that's why, in this ongoing relationship I appreciate sections like I Cor. 13, and Ps. 139—you just can't escape God's love."

—Steve McMaster, Bartonsville, Penn.[4]

How will you handle it?

If you are interested in bridging the so-called generation gap or relevance gap between the church and society, the following questionnaire can give you a start. Apply it to your own church, your own youth group, wherever you are joining other believers in service for Christ.

1. Does Jesus Christ and His work really come first?
2. Are we trying to accomplish something, even with the most ordinary, routine procedures, or are we just going through a routine?
3. Are we satisfied with the status quo? Or do we feel honest guilt and repentance about our lack of impact?
4. How many of us are giving *110%?* How many of us think we are giving 50%? How many are willing to try for 110%?

5. How do we see our leisure time? As something that should be jealously guarded for ourselves? Is the way we use our leisure time helping us become stronger in Christ or are we getting pressed into the mold?

6. What about our concern with details? Are we prepared to do something for Christ or do we just think we know a lot about theology and religion? Do we put on sharp, well-planned programs and events with a specific spiritual goal or do we play it by ear or fly by the seat of our pants and just meet to be meeting?

7. Are we accomplishing anything?

8. Are we willing to admit our problems? Or do we try to keep hiding behind a pious, phony facade and convince one another that Christ has solved all our problems?

9. Do we work and think as a team or are we willing to let the superstars in our church do most of the job?

10. Is each one of us willing to serve to the best of his ability and is each of us being allowed to do this?

The above questionnaire is based on Paul's advice to Timothy (2 Tim. 2:3-5). You may want to apply it to yourself before using it with your group.

But individually and collectively, it's time for Christians to take a choice.

Joshua said to God's people, ". . . if it does not please you to worship the LORD, choose here and now whom you will worship . . ." (Josh. 24:15, *New English Bible*).

Elijah told the Israelites, "How long will you sit on the fence? If the Lord is God, follow Him; but if Baal, then follow him" (1 Kings 18:21, *New English Bible*).

And Jesus said (in Matt. 6:24, *New English Bible*): "No servant can be the slave of two masters; for either he will hate the first and love the second, or he will be devoted to the first and think nothing of the second. You cannot serve God and Money."

The GeNeRaTioN GaP[5]

Mary: Another Sunday, and here I am in church again
. . . funny how I don't get bored with it like I used to . . .
oh, there's old Mrs. Langford! She's really a pillar of the
church . . . nearly eighty years old, and she still comes
every Sunday and gives money and support to the youth
program . . .

Mrs. Langford: I really feel at home here in the chapel,
even though Mr. Langford can't come . . . I know he's with
Jesus. He was the best husband . . . oh, there's that
young Peterson girl smiling at me . . . she's a fine girl.
Her kind will build the church in years to come, as she
gets older . . .

Mary: It's time for the Scripture reading . . . I sure
like my new English translation; it really zeroes in on my
life and lays God's Word on me . . . it helps me to understand when they read the King James Version, too . . .

Mrs. Langford: I know that King James isn't completely understood by everyone, but it's so musical and beautiful to read . . . it isn't so very hard to understand for those of us who read it a lot . . . I rather prefer it to all these new translations . . .

Mary: Now the hymn is beginning . . . we young people find some of these lines hard to understand, like "Here I raise mine Ebenezer" . . . last week at the youth meeting they sang "Land Without Tears" . . . I could dig that; it speaks my language . . . for first choice I'll take the more lively songs . . . the beat can't hide the pure beauty of God's salvation through Jesus Christ . . .

Mrs. Langford: The good old hymns . . . they're so stately and grand . . . and they say exactly what I feel . . . they might last for another century, because they get across the basic salvation plan, and no song can do more than that . . .

Mary: The pastor's getting ready to speak now . . . he's pretty smart for an older guy . . . sometimes when he preaches to the kids he really wakes me up . . . it almost scares me when I realize how little I've done for Christ, and He's coming so soon . . . lots of my friends could be left behind . . . oh, it's time for silent prayer . . .

Mrs. Langford: Here's the pastor now . . . he's really a deep thinker, for a younger fellow . . . I don't think this new generation is going to do so badly after all . . . anyway, he's clearing his throat to speak, so I'll open my Bible . . . oh, but first time for silent prayer, of course . . .

"O Lord, help me to realize that there are other viewpoints besides mine. You can be as big as this world or as narrow as my mind. Keep me open-minded and speak to me as the pastor speaks, guiding me in Your love and power and opening my eyes. Thank You for Your patience and forgiveness. In Jesus' name. Amen."

184

ReSOURceS aND BIBLIOGRAPHY

CHAPTER 1

1. Quoted in the *New York Times,* August 5, 1966, p. 20.
2. "The Way It Starts," *Campus Life,* October, 1969, p. 31.

CHAPTER 2

1. This anecdote is based on the article, "The Ministry of Doubt," Rev. Elmer L. Towns, *Evangelical Beacon,* September 28, 1965.
2. See "The Ministry of Doubt," Elmer L. Towns, *Evangelical Beacon,* September 28, 1965.
3. See "Who Is the King of Glory?" Gertrude Haan, *Christianity Today,* December 8, 1967.
4. "Smash into Frustrations," *Campus Life,* October, 1969, p. 35.
5. See "Doubters Welcome," Charles Hummel, *HIS* magazine, January, 1964, p. 11.
6. See "No Doubt," Hubert Butcher, *HIS* magazine, February, 1969, p. 23.
7. "Doubters Welcome," *HIS* magazine, January, 1964, p. 11.

CHAPTER 3

1. Testimony of Chris Xenakis, *Collegiate Challenge,* vol. 9, no. 1, p. 11.
2. *Between God and Satan,* Helmut Thielicke, Wm. B. Eerdmans Publishing Co., translation copyright, 1958, Oliver & Boyd, pp. 18, 19.

CHAPTER 4

1. Twenty-four years old at the time she wrote this testimony, Coni had spent seven years moving with the fast crowd in her high school and elsewhere. Coni found Christ in 1970, and joined the Christian World Liberation Front in Berkeley, California. Her testimony appeared in *Focus on Youth,* official publication of Young Life, vol. 4, no. 2, Summer, 1970. Used by permission.

CHAPTER 5

1. True experience related by Bruce Larson in his book *Setting Men Free,* copyright 1967, Donovan Publishing House, pp. 69, 70.
2. "With People It's Different Now," *Campus Life,* October, 1969, p. 38.
3. *The Gospel of Luke,* translated and interpreted by William Barclay. Published by The Saint Andrew Press, Edinburgh, 1953; and in the U.S.A. by Westminster Press, 1954, p. 37.

CHAPTER 6

1. Credited to Johann Heinrich Heidigger, a seventeenth century theologian and philosopher.
2. Lynn's story is a true account. The daughter of missionary parents, she is now married and has an effective Christian ministry as a writer and teacher.
3. "This Guy Talks Like He'll Live Forever," Gordon MacLean, *Campus Life,* August/September, 1970.
4. "The Door to His Place," Georgiana Walker, Associate Editor, Gospel Light Publications.

CHAPTER 7

1. Excerpted from an actual letter by a teen-ager named Debby published in *Spirit* magazine, June, 1967. See p. 15.

2. *Who Moved the Stone?*, Frank Morison. Published 1930, Faber & Faber, Ltd., 1962, by Barnes & Noble, Inc., p. 11.

3. From the poem, "Faith" by John Oxenham, *Bees in Amber*, copyright 1959, Fleming H. Revell Co., p. 105.

4. See "In the Spirit of Advice," *Spirit*, September, 1967, pp. 7-9.

5. "How I Know," *Campus Life*, October, 1969, p. 32.

CHAPTER 8

1. According to Jewish dietary laws found in Leviticus 11, the Jew can only eat animals which chew the cud or animals with cloven hoofs—cow, goat, etc. All other animals—to the Jews at least—were called unclean and forbidden. A typical example would be the hog.

2. See *The Acts of the Apostles*, translated and interpreted by William Barclay. Published by The Saint Andrew Press, Edinburgh, 1953; and in the U.S.A. by Westminster Press, 1955, p. 84.

3. Lew Alcindor's engrossing autobiography appeared in three installments, "My Story," J. Olsen, *Sports Illustrated* magazine, Oct. 27, Nov. 3, Nov. 10, 1969.

4. "It's My World and I want to Be Part of the Answer," *Campus Life*, October, 1969, p. 36.

5. For a candid discussion of prejudice, see "Campus Life Forum," *Campus Life*, June/July, 1970, p. 7.

CHAPTER 9

1. Based on *The Four Spiritual Laws* published by Campus Crusade for Christ International, Arrowhead Springs, San Bernardino, California.

2. "I Gotta Stop for Fuel," Lonnie Royal, *Campus Life*, October, 1969, p. 41.

CHAPTER 10

1. "Spotless," Milo Kaufmann, *Youth Christian Companion*. Reprinted in *HIS*, October, 1965; *Campus Life*, ——————, Copyright 1964.

2. These ideas on witnessing adapted from the article "Doin' Your Thing!" *Campus Life*, July, 1968, pp. 18–20.

CHAPTER 11

1. If you are interested in reading more regarding the helping role and its relationship to psychology or education, see *On Becoming a Person* and *Client Centered Therapy*, both by Carl Rogers, Houghton Mifflin Company.

2. *Tough Love*, Bill Milliken, with Char Meredith, Fleming H. Revell, 1968, p. 131. Used by permission.

CHAPTER 12

1. "A Student's Open Letter to God," David R. Knighton, *Christianity Today*, June 5, 1970, p. 16.

2. "A Word to the Now Generation," Joseph Bayly, *Eternity* magazine, March, 1967. Reprinted by permission.

3. Material on George Allen's "Ten Commandments" adapted from "Ram Coach Lives, Works by Demanding Code," Bob Oates, *Los Angeles Times*, July 9, 1970.

4. "This Is Just the Beginning," *Campus Life*, October, 1969, pp. 143,144.

5. "Generation Gap," Scott Pinzon.

The publishers do not necessarily endorse the entire contents of all publications referred to in this book.